W9-BLO-015

RUBELLA AND RUBEOLA

DEADLY DISEASES AND EPIDEMICS

DEADLY DISEASES AND EPIDEMICS

RUBELLA AND RUBEOLA

Brian R. Shmaefsky, Ph.D.

CONSULTING EDITOR
Hilary Babcock, M.D., M.P.H.,
Infectious Diseases Division,
Washington University School of Medicine,
Medical Director of Occupational Health (Infectious Diseases),
Barnes-Jewish Hospital and St. Louis Children's Hospital

FOREWORD BY
David Heymann
World Health Organization

CHELSEA HOUSE
PUBLISHERS
An imprint of Infobase Publishing

Rubella and Rubeola

Chelsea House
An imprint of Infobase Publishing
132 West 31st Street
New York NY 10001

Library of Congress Cataloging-in-Publication Data
Shmaefsky, Brian.
  Rubella and rubeola / Brian R. Shmaefsky ; consulting editor, Hilary Babcock ; foreword by David Heymann.
    p. cm. — (Deadly diseases and epidemics)
  Includes bibliographical references and index.
  ISBN-13: 978-1-60413-230-4 (alk. paper)
  ISBN-10: 1-60413-230-2 (alk. paper)
  1. Rubella—Popular works. 2. Measles—Popular works. I. Title. II. Series.
  RA644.R8S63 2009
  614.5'24—dc22

Chelsea House books are available at special discounts when purchased in bulk quantities for businesses, associations, institutions, or sales promotions. Please call our Special Sales Department in New York at (212) 967-8800 or (800) 322-8755.

You can find Chelsea House on the World Wide Web at http://www.chelseahouse.com

Series design by Terry Mallon
Cover design by Takeshi Takahashi

Printed in the United States of America

Bang FOF 10 9 8 7 6 5 4 3 2 1

This book is printed on acid-free paper.

All links and Web addresses were checked and verified to be correct at the time of publication. Because of the dynamic nature of the Web, some addresses and links may have changed since publication and may no longer be valid.

Table of Contents

Foreword

Communicable diseases kill and cause long-term disability. The microbial agents that cause them are dynamic, changeable, and resilient: They are responsible for more than 14 million deaths each year, mainly in developing countries.

Approximately 46 percent of all deaths in the developing world are due to communicable diseases, and almost 90 percent of these deaths are from AIDS, tuberculosis, malaria, and acute diarrheal and respiratory infections of children. In addition to causing great human suffering, these high-mortality communicable diseases have become major obstacles to economic development. They are a challenge to control either because of the lack of effective vaccines, or because the drugs that are used to treat them are becoming less effective because of antimicrobial drug resistance.

Millions of people, especially those who are poor and living in developing countries, are also at risk from disabling communicable diseases such as polio, leprosy, lymphatic filariasis, and onchocerciasis. In addition to human suffering and permanent disability, these communicable diseases create an economic burden—both on the workforce that handicapped persons are unable to join, and on their families and society, upon which they must often depend for economic support.

Finally, the entire world is at risk of the unexpected communicable diseases, those that are called emerging or re-emerging infections. Infection is often unpredictable because risk factors for transmission are not understood, or because it often results from organisms that cross the species barrier from animals to humans. The cause is often viral, such as Ebola and Marburg hemorrhagic fevers and severe acute respiratory syndrome (SARS). In addition to causing human suffering and death, these infections place health workers at great risk and are costly to economies. Infections such as Bovine Spongiform Encephalopathy (BSE) and the associated new human variant of Creutzfeldt-Jakob Disease (vCJD) in Europe, and avian influenza A (H5N1) in Asia, are reminders of the seriousness of emerging and re-emerging infections. In addition, many of these infections have the potential to cause pandemics, which are a constant threat to our economies and public health security.

Science has given us vaccines and anti-infective drugs that have helped keep infectious diseases under control. Nothing demonstrates the effectiveness of vaccines better than the successful eradication of smallpox, the decrease in polio as the eradication program continues, and the decrease in measles when routine immunization programs are supplemented by mass vaccination campaigns.

Likewise, the effectiveness of anti-infective drugs is clearly demonstrated through prolonged life or better health in those infected with viral diseases such as AIDS, parasitic infections such as malaria, and bacterial infections such as tuberculosis and pneumococcal pneumonia.

But current research and development is not filling the pipeline for new anti-infective drugs as rapidly as resistance is developing, nor is vaccine development providing vaccines for some of the most common and lethal communicable diseases. At the same time, providing people with access to existing anti-infective drugs, vaccines, and goods such as condoms or bed nets—necessary for the control of communicable diseases in many developing countries—remains a great challenge.

Education, experimentation, and the discoveries that grow from them are the tools needed to combat high mortality infectious diseases, diseases that cause disability, or emerging and re-emerging infectious diseases. At the same time, partnerships between developing and industrialized countries can overcome many of the challenges of access to goods and technologies. This book may inspire its readers to set out on the path of drug and vaccine development, or on the path to discovering better public health technologies by applying our current understanding of the human genome and those of various infectious agents. Readers may likewise be inspired to help ensure wider access to those protective goods and technologies. Such inspiration, with pragmatic action, will keep us on the winning side of the struggle against communicable diseases.

David L. Heymann
Assistant Director General
Health Security and Environment
Representative of the Director General for Polio Eradication
World Health Organization
Geneva, Switzerland

1
Viral Diseases

Nobody seemed to be safe from the disease. It affected all people, but it seemed to be more common in families and people working in close quarters. The disease caused the afflicted peoples' bodies to be covered with blood-colored sores. Plus, they complained of being tired and chilled. All the afflicted said that they had a sore throat and were coughing before feeling truly ill. This new type of plague seemed to disappear from the population as fast as it appeared. It came in big bouts sometimes three or four times a year. Yet the severity of the disease seemed to vary with each occurrence. Eighth-century Iranian physician Abu Bakr Muhammad Ibn Zakariya al-Razi observed this in his practice and read accounts like this from other physicians living in the Middle East in the eighth century. Little did he know that he was making observations that would help him identify the diseases now known as rubeola and rubella.

THE HISTORY OF VIRUSES

The diseases commonly called red measles (rubeola) and German measles (rubella) are caused by two unrelated viruses. Viruses are intracellular parasites that must carry out their life cycles using the resources of another organism's cells. Unlike many diseases, viruses usually infect only a specific type of organism. So, viruses that cause disease in fish would not likely harm humans. Viruses also infect only particular types of cells in an organism. For example, a cold virus can only infect cells of the respiratory system and cannot invade cells of other body organs.

Diseases that were caused by viruses were familiar to people long before the nature of viruses was discovered. Evidence of an ailment similar to the viral disease poliomyelitis (polio) was recorded on an Egyptian hieroglyph from approximately 3700 B.C. Medical evidence of another viral disease was found on the mummy of Pharaoh Ramses V, who died in 1196 B.C. Scarring on the preserved skin of his face and body was consistent with smallpox.

From the 1890s through the 1940s, researchers debated the nature of viruses. Some scientists thought that viruses were poisons that dissolved into the cell and caused disease. Other researchers assumed viruses were minute intracellular bacteria-like organisms that were too small to detect. The idea that viruses were a unique life form came about in 1892, when Russian botanist Dimitri Ivanovski unknowingly discovered that a common tobacco disease was caused by a virus. He determined this by **filtering** the diseased tobacco tissues in an attempt to isolate the organism causing the disease. Ivanovski was surprised to learn that the disease organism was smaller than any known cell. Other scientists did similar studies on other diseases and called the disease organisms unfilterable infectious **agents**. In 1898, Dutch microbiologist Martinus Beijerinck became the first person to use the term *virus* to describe these pathogens that were smaller than bacteria.

Viruses started to become associated with a variety of diseases in the early 1900s. In 1911, American physician Peyton Rous revealed a virus in chickens that caused cancerous **tumors**. This discovery paved the way for modern cancer research and a better understanding of how viruses induce disease. Using Rous's chicken virus, scientists discovered that certain cancers of the blood and reproductive tract caused cells to become cancerous. Another great moment in **virology** came about in 1937 when Max Theiler of South Africa was able to culture viruses in chicken eggs. He used the cells of the developing chick as a medium for replicating the viruses, since viruses can only replicate in living cells and cannot be cultivated using artificial conditions. This was a fascinating achievement considering that scientists knew very little about the structure and life cycle of viruses.

A LIFE FORM SIMPLER THAN A VIRUS?

The discovery of viruses reinvented the way biologists view life. Viruses have almost none of the typical characteristics of other living organisms. However, viruses do possess genetic material, which is a fundamental feature needed for the maintenance and reproduction of all organisms. Viruses primarily use their genetic material for replication.

A new type of disease particle was more recently implicated in a variety of diseases that cause brain decay in animals and humans. In 1936, a sheep disease called scrapie was thought to be caused by an elusive virus called a "slow virus." A slow virus was believed to be a small piece of DNA that hid within the DNA of its host cell. This made it almost impossible to collect and study slow viruses. A variety of other diseases were then associated with slow viruses even though they were never isolated from the infected cells.

In 1982, American scientist Stanley Prusiner claimed to have found the virus-like agent researchers were calling a slow virus. It turned out that he discovered a life form that was composed only of a simple protein. Prusiner called this new disease agent a *prion*. He came up with the name by combining the first two syllables of the words *protein* and *infectious*. Many researchers now use the abbreviation PrP to refer to the prion protein. Prusiner's claim met with much criticism from the scientific community. Other scientists did not agree with Prusiner's explanation of prion replication. It was thought that only nucleic acids were capable of replication. Prusiner was awarded the 1997 Nobel Prize in Physiology or Medicine for his discovery. A wealth of current research studies has since convinced the scientific community about prion replication. Prions are now accepted as a new type of infectious particle by the scientific community. Diseases caused by prions are collectively known as transmissible spongiform encephalopathies and include Creutzfeldt-Jakob Disease (CJD) and kuru.

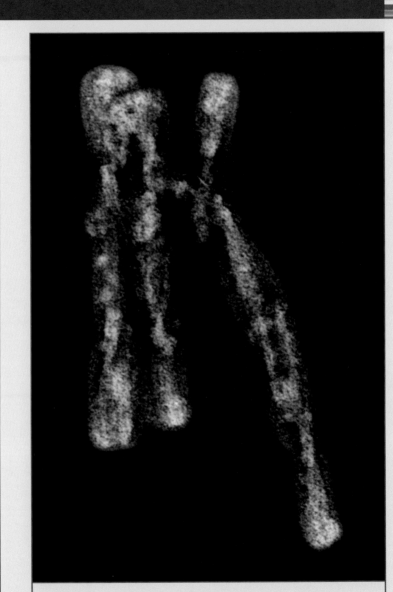

Figure 1.1 This is an electron microscope image of the prion that causes Creutzfeldt-Jakob Disease (CJD). (© Science VU/Stanly B. Prusiner/Visuals Unlimited)

Figure 1.2 Peyton Rous, shown here at his microscope, expanded the scientific understanding of how viruses cause disease. (Courtesy National Library of Medicine/U.S. National Institutes of Health)

By the 1940s, new advances in biology and chemistry gave scientists insight into the chemical structure of viruses. They learned that most viruses were composed simply of **proteins** and **nucleic acids**. Proteins are complex molecules made up of amino acids that are needed for cell structure and function. Nucleic acids are complex molecules associated with the structure and function of genetic material. **DNA** and **RNA** are composed of nucleic acids. It was also in the 1940s that the first virus was photographed using an **electron microscope**, a powerful microscope that uses **electrons** to magnify an object. The nature of viral life cycles remained elusive until the 1950s. Between 1940 and 1953, a series of independent epic studies by Martha Chase, Max Delbruck, Alfred Hershey, Joshua Lederberg, Salvador Luria, and Norton Zinder elucidated viral replication. They worked out the life cycle of a simple virus called a **bacteriophage**. Bacteriophages infect bacteria. All of these scientists were awarded Nobel Prizes for their contributions to the study of viral disease.

WHAT'S IN A NAME?

The history of how viruses got to be called "viruses" is very elusive. The coining of the term *virus* as a name for the unfilterable infectious agents is not attributed to one person or one scientific study. People in Europe started using the term *virus* in 1392 to refer to diseases caused by "venomous substances." These venomous substances were thought to be produced by unclean habits or thoughts. The term *virus* is Latin for several things. It means "poison," "sap of plants," or "slimy liquid." *Virus* is related to the Greek words *ios*, which means "poison," and *ixos*, which means "mistletoe." The first recorded use of *virus* to explain certain diseases was in 1728. Scientists used the term to mean an "agent that causes infectious disease." The adjective form *viral* was used in the scientific literature starting in 1948. Physicians and scientists use a similar term *virulent* when describing aggressive diseases caused by any microorganism. Virulent means "extremely infectious or poisonous." It dates back to the Latin word *virulentus*, which means "poisonous."

Biologists today do not categorize viruses with other living organisms. Unlike other organisms, viruses cannot carry out major life functions such as adaptation, **metabolism**, and reproduction. The conventional definition of living organisms includes these functions. Viruses are now called **particles** because they are organism-like things that do not possess the major properties of life. They even lack the genetic information to conduct any living processes.

WHAT IS A VIRUS?

There is no "typical" virus. Viruses vary greatly in structure and life cycle. Any description of a "typical" virus is based on the structure and life cycle of the T series of bacteriophages. These viruses were first identified in 1896 by English biologist Ernest Hankin, who discovered the ability of T series bacteriophages to kill bacteria in water from the Ganges and Jumna Rivers in India. Bacteriophages were made available for study after they were isolated by Frederick Twort in 1915 and cultured in the laboratory by French Canadian biologist Felix d'Herelle in 1917. T series bacteriophages were the subject of the most influential viral research studies from the 1940s through the 1960s.

In 1935 American biologist Wendell Stanley proved that viruses were simple organisms that lack a cell structure. He turned a tobacco virus into a compact **crystal**, indicating that is was composed of a parcel of simple **molecules** that make up other organisms. The procedure he used was called **crystallography**. Another technique called electron microscopy was used to determine the structure of a virus by German physician Helmuth Ruska in 1940. He confirmed that a virus has no cell structure and that it resembles a simple assemblage of molecules with no obvious evidence of living properties.

It is now known that most viruses are composed of genetic material enclosed in a protein **casing** called a capsid. The genetic material is called the **genome** and can be composed of

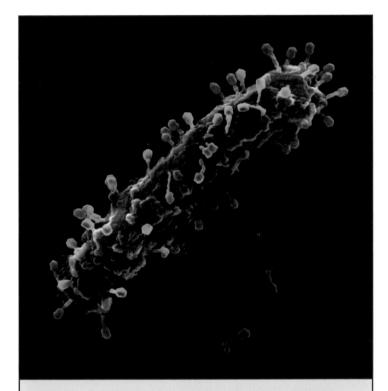

Figure 1.3 These T series bacteriophages are attacking an *Escherichia coli* bacterium. These bacteriophages will attach to the bacterium and use their tails to inject their DNA into the bacterium. This will force the *E. coli* bacterium to reproduce more bacteriophages. (© Eye of Science/Photo Researchers, Inc.)

DNA or RNA. All other known organisms use DNA as their genetic material; RNA is usually used to assist with the function of DNA.

THE CAPSID

Capsids come in various shapes and sizes; most often they are shaped like boxes or spirals. The main job of the capsid is to protect the viral genome from damage. Various conditions in the environment that can damage the viral genome include

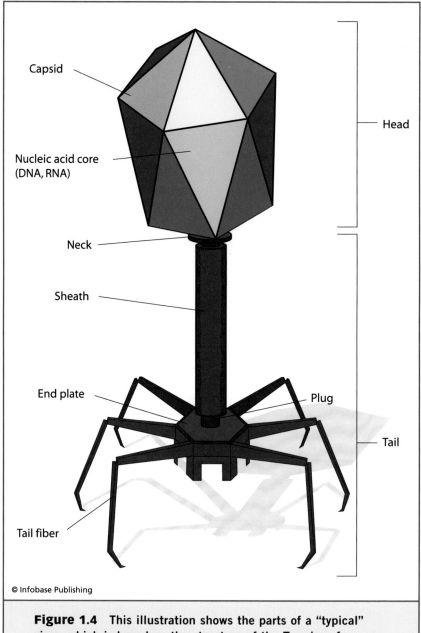

Capsid

Nucleic acid core
(DNA, RNA)

Neck

Sheath

End plate

Tail fiber

Head

Plug

Tail

© Infobase Publishing

Figure 1.4 This illustration shows the parts of a "typical" virus, which is based on the structure of the T series of bacteriophages.

corrosive chemicals, **enzymes**, and **ultraviolet light**. Corrosive chemicals break apart or wear away materials gradually by chemical action. Enzymes are proteins that carry out specific chemical reactions. Enzymes produced by bacteria and other organisms can break down unprotected viral genomes. Ultraviolet light is a high-energy light that can damage many types of molecules, including DNA and RNA.

The capsid of most viruses is made up of similar protein subunits that lock together to form the casing. These subunit proteins are generally called **capsomeres**. The suffix -*mere* means "a piece of." Capsomeres have two unique characteristics that facilitate replication of the virus. The capsomeres lock together to form structures in a manner similar to building blocks. A particular capsomere shape and arrangement can produce a specific form to the capsid. Most viruses are composed of identical capsomeres that form the final capsid shape. The capsomeres are also **self-assembling**, which means that they can form complex structures on their own accord by attaching to one another or to other chemicals.

Capsids contain other types of proteins. Many of these proteins help the virus complete its life cycle, which comprises infecting cells and then replicating themselves. These proteins are commonly called virus **attachment proteins**. At first scientists called these proteins **antigens**. An antigen is any substance that can produce an **immune response**. American biologist George Hirst discovered antigens in 1941 when he noticed blood responding to the viral antigen as part of an immune response. Attachment proteins help viruses find and insert themselves into cells. The attachment proteins restrict the types of organisms and cells a virus can invade.

Many viruses have complex capsid forms. For example, bacteriophages resemble small machines with legs designed to land on a cell and a needle-like protein projection called a tail fiber that is designed for inserting the viral genome into the cell. Some more complex viruses have an inner capsid that directly surrounds the genome. This structure is called the **nucleocap-sid**. Nucleocapsid proteins are distinct from capsid proteins and self-assemble around the viral genome. Research studies show that the nucleocapsid protects the genome of viruses, which would otherwise rapidly destabilize and decay.

Certain viruses have a capsid surrounded by a structure that resembles a **cell membrane**. Viruses that possess this covering are called **enveloped viruses**. Scientists humorously coined the term *naked virus* to describe viruses lacking an **envelope**. The envelope is composed of components from the infected cell and virus capsid. Enveloped viruses acquire part of the cell membrane when they exit the infected cell after replicating. This "stolen" portion of the cell membrane now becomes the envelope. The virus then incorporates attachment proteins and other types of proteins into the envelope. Research studies show that the envelope protects the virus from drying and from enzymes that are capable of breaking down proteins and nucleic acids. The envelope also assists the virus in entering host cells. Certain enveloped viruses contain enzymes that help them become established quickly in cells that they invade.

GENETIC MATERIAL

Viral genetic material is as variable as viral capsids. The characteristics of the viral genome are a major factor is classifying viruses. Viral genomes are first categorized by the composition of their genome. The genome can be either DNA or RNA. **DNA viruses** contain a DNA genome, and **RNA viruses** contain an RNA genome. DNA viruses can have DNA that is either **double-stranded** or **single-stranded**. Double-stranded DNA is made up of two chains of nucleic acids attached side-by-side. Single-stranded DNA is made up of only one chain of nucleic acids. The strands of DNA can be linear (in a straight line) or circular. Double-stranded circular DNA is the most stable form of DNA and is difficult to break down.

RNA viruses can also be double-stranded or single-stranded. Single-stranded RNA viruses can be classified as **positive-sense RNA** or **negative-sense RNA**. Positive-sense RNA viruses replicate in two steps. The cell first builds a DNA blueprint of the viral DNA. It then directly replicates the positive-sense RNA from the DNA blueprint. The replication of negative-sense RNA viruses is very complex compared to DNA viruses and positive-sense RNA viruses. They go through a step in which the cell must make negative-sense RNA after creating a DNA blueprint and a positive-sense RNA.

HOW DO VIRUSES REPLICATE?

Viruses cause disease when they infect cells for the purpose of replicating. A virus does not reproduce like other organisms. All other organisms either use a process called cell division to replicate cells, or they make **gametes** for **sexual reproduction**. Viruses must have a host cell to carry out replication. The virus reproduces by using the host cell to manufacture viral components. The virus's genome carries just enough information to take control of the host cell and direct the cell to replicate the virus.

Replication for most viruses involves seven steps that result in the production of hundreds to thousands of replicated viruses in each host cell. Viruses have no living properties when outside of a host cell. Almost all viruses must be able to find a host cell before their genome decays. Dehydration and corrosive chemicals can damage the capsid, which protects the genome from being degraded. Single-stranded genomes are unstable and decay readily. Double-stranded genomes are a bit tougher, but can be broken down by corrosive chemicals, enzymes from bodily fluids and microorganisms, and sunlight. The time a virus can sit intact in the environment varies greatly with the type of virus and with the environmental conditions. Under favorable environmental conditions, some viruses are inactivated after several hours, whereas others may remain intact for days. Viruses can remain undamaged for decades in continuously frozen environments sheltered from the sun.

THE LIFE CYCLE OF A VIRUS

The first step of the viral life cycle is transmission to a host cell. Transmission is a critical step because the virus must make it to a new host organism before the virus is damaged. Viruses completely rely on the host organism to carry out the means of transmission. In many situations, some activity of the host organism directly transfers the virus to another organism. Certain viruses are transmitted to a new host by a vector. In complex animals and plants, viruses are transmitted from cell to cell within the body as well as transferred to a new host. Successful transmission means that the virus must make contact with uninfected host cell. For most viruses, this means that the virus must enter the body and be transferred to the particular cells that they infect. For example, the hepatitis virus must be able to reach liver cells in order to replicate.

Following the transmission step is the **adsorption** step, which involves the virus's attachment to the host cell's surface. Attachment typically occurs on particular cells of the host. Attachment takes place when viruses come across a cell that has cell membrane **receptors** that match the viral attachment proteins. Many types of receptors are found on the outer surface of the cell membrane. Receptors carry out many functions for a cell, including the detection of certain chemicals such as **hormones**. Viruses cannot seek out a particular receptor. They are transmitted randomly to host cells and by chance may reach a cell that matches their attachment proteins.

After adsorption, the viral infection progresses to the third stage, which is called penetration. Viruses without an envelope stimulate the cell to engulf the virus. These viruses attach to a specific cell receptor that causes the cell to take in the virus. Cells engulf viruses by covering the virus with a bubble of cell membrane. The cell then moves the bubble into the cell,

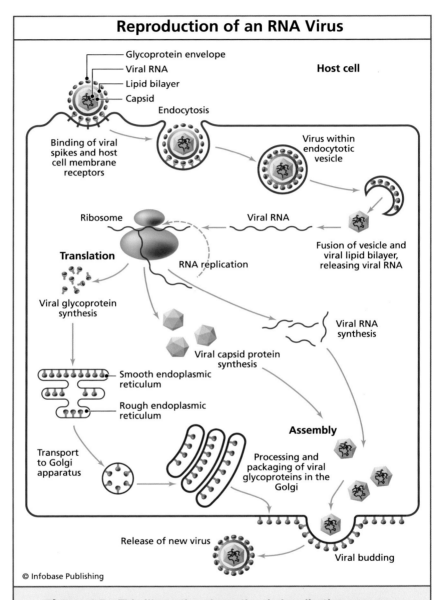

Reproduction of an RNA Virus

Glycoprotein envelope
Viral RNA
Lipid bilayer
Capsid
Endocytosis

Host cell

Binding of viral spikes and host cell membrane receptors

Virus within endocytotic vesicle

Ribosome

Viral RNA

Translation

RNA replication

Fusion of vesicle and viral lipid bilayer, releasing viral RNA

Viral glycoprotein synthesis

Viral RNA synthesis

Viral capsid protein synthesis

Smooth endoplasmic reticulum

Rough endoplasmic reticulum

Assembly

Transport to Golgi apparatus

Processing and packaging of viral glycoproteins in the Golgi

Release of new virus

Viral budding

© Infobase Publishing

Figure 1.5   This illustration shows the viral replication process. First, the virus enters a host cell. The virus then sheds its protein coat to begin replication using the host cell's genetic material. After the new copies of the virus have been put together, they are released from the cell.

swallowing up the virus. Enveloped viruses enter a cell by fusing with the cell membrane. Upon fusion, the virus either blends with the cell or is engulfed in a bubble of cell membrane. The virus is not yet active at this point of infection.

Stage four of infection is the **uncoating** event. At this stage the envelope and capsid break apart, releasing the viral genome into the intracellular fluids. Viral replication cannot take place without this stage. Researchers have discovered that once the virus is uncoated, it is very difficult to find the viral genome in the host cell. Thus, scientists call this the **eclipse phase** because the virus is apparently hiding in the cell. At this stage it is possible for the cell to destroy the virus using enzymes and other molecules designed to ward off viral attack. Cells attack viruses using proteins and nucleic acids that digest viral genetic material.

The next stage is called **synthesis**; at this stage the cell is being directed by the virus to replicate the viral genome and capsomeres. This stage varies greatly. Each virus has a specific synthesis stage based on its genome composition and type of capsid. The viral genome serves as the blueprint for building the viral components. Overall, many viruses start the synthesis stage by first producing repressor proteins that control certain host cell functions. At this point, the cell is now diseased and does not carry out many of its vital functions. Some cells die prematurely at this stage and in turn stop viral replication. In humans, infected cells usually release signaling proteins that initiate an immune response targeted at controlling viral replication.

Viral assembly is the sixth stage of infection. It is some-times called the **maturation phase**. This is when the viral parts come together inside the infected cell to form new viruses. Multiple copies of new genomes are made using the cell's chemistry for making DNA and RNA from nucleic acid building blocks in the cell. These copies then bind to viral proteins to combine the genome copies with capsomeres. The replicated capsomere proteins self-assemble around the genome or the nucleocapsid. Other proteins are also made by the host cell and self-assembled into the capsid structure. Many of the mature viruses contain defects, including incomplete genomes and abnormal capsids. The number of defective viruses is insignificant compared to the number of normal viruses that will move along successfully to the last stage of infection.

The **release phase** is the final stage of viral infection. Like the synthesis stage, this stage varies greatly among the different types of viruses. Some viruses are released from the cell by programming the cell to undergo **lysis**, which causes the cell to break down and die. The cell can be induced into lysis by specific viral proteins. In many cases, a cell undergoes lysis as it slowly dies over the course of the viral infection. Other viruses remain in the cell for long periods of time without reaching the release phase. In certain cases, these delayed viruses can cause a cell to replicate rapidly and produce a tumor. It is possible for some tumors to develop into cancer.

Certain enveloped viruses bud from the cell. The virus forms a bud by being pushed against the inner surface of the cell until it becomes enveloped in a bubble of cell membrane. The bud is then released, and this produces a viral capsid surrounded by an envelope that is composed of cell membrane and viral proteins. Enveloped viruses usually bud slowly, which keeps the cell alive for the natural lifetime of the cell and produces a persistent infection that results in a long illness.

Much of the illness associated with a viral infection is due to a loss of cell function. Viral replication prevents the cell from carrying out its functions. Some of these cell functions may affect the rest of the body. Viruses that infect cells of critical body organs can produce severe effects on the body and can lead to death.

The time it takes to feel ill from a viral infection depends on the replication speed of the virus. A certain number of cells must be infected before the body is affected by the nonfunctioning

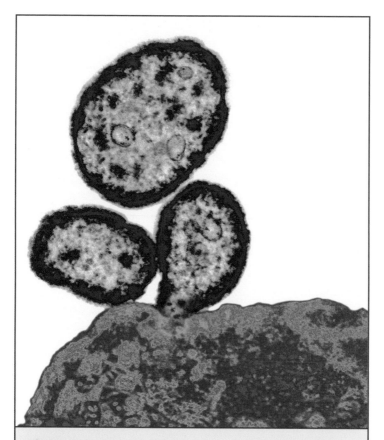

Figure 1.6 Here is a rubeola virus budding from a cell membrane. When an enveloped virus such as this one forms inside a cell, it pushes against the inner surface of the host cell until it is surrounded by the host cell's membrane. When the bud is released from the host cell, the viral capsid has an envelope that is composed of a combination of the host cell's membrane and viral proteins. (© Dr. Hans Gelderblom/ Visuals Unlimited)

cells. Other **signs** and **symptoms** of viral infections are caused by the immune system's reaction to the infection. Many viruses cause the immune system to release chemicals that produce fever, a runny nose, rashes, tiredness, and watery eyes. Various other chemicals produced by the immune system can accidentally kill healthy cells as the body is attacking the cells invaded with viruses

Viruses are highly efficient organisms that rapidly spread from one host to the next in their attempt to survive. They reproduce rapidly and are able to exit the body well before the immune system can get rid of the invasion. Most viruses are only able to infect one particular type of organism. However, many viruses can be spread from one organism to another, causing a different type of disease in the new host. It is typical for viruses to invade a particular body region. The measles viruses are usually restricted to human hosts and are capable of spreading to a variety of body parts.

2

An Ancient "Plague"

Each year in Pakistan, more than 2 million cases of a notorious ancient plague occur every year. Approximately 12,000 of these cases are children from the Punjab region of Pakistan who die from this plague. This plague is the familiar disease known as rubeola. In 2005, the Pakistani government implemented a program to track the spread of disease among the approximately 63 million Pakistani children between the ages of 9 months and 13 years. The Pakistani government wanted to develop a strategy for decreasing the incidence of rubeola using vaccines in areas susceptible to the disease. It was hoped that, if caught early, measles would no longer be a deadly plague in Pakistan.

WHAT IS A PLAGUE?

The two diseases collectively known as measles were at one time called a "plague." Before the 1600s, the word *plague* referred to some sort of infestation of annoyances, diseases, or troubles. Many people even viewed a string of bad luck or misfortune as a plague. Modern European languages after the 1600s focused the meaning of *plague* to apply to some type of event or incident that caused anguish. Today, it is commonly used to refer to some types of infectious disease.

The word *plague* seems to have originated in the ancient Greek and Roman languages. In Greek, the term *plaga* meant "to strike or hit." The Latin word *plangere* referred to a wound caused by a strike. In both languages, the word evolved to mean having a condition that causes a person to "lament" or "grieve."

A typical plague brought grieving to the individual as well as to the community. Plagues were not necessarily events that affected large populations or occurred without warning. The ancient Greeks sometimes used the term *plague* to explain **genetic disorders** that may have affected a single person or family. However, most of the noteworthy plagues recorded in historical records caused widespread illness or death. This is the most familiar use of the word, referring to diseases that have some obvious effect such as discoloration and disfigurement or that produce extreme suffering and inevitable death.

Animals and plants were also the victims of plagues. Conditions afflicting agricultural and domesticated animals and plants, however, are usually called blights. Blights most often occur due to outbreaks of diseases caused by **microorganisms** such as bacteria, fungi, and viruses. Microorganisms include microscopic organisms composed usually of a single cell. A cell is the smallest unit of life that makes up an organism. The term *blight* was used throughout Europe by farmers after the early 1600s. It is believed to derive from the Old English word *blaece*, which was a skin condition caused by tuberculosis. (Tuberculosis is a bacterial disease of humans that affects the lungs, bones, and skin.) The word *blaece* is similar to the Old Norse term *blikna*, which means "to become pale," such as happens with the tuberculosis skin disease.

It is not unusual to come across the term *blight* when explaining plagues. In the 1800s, *blight* and *plague* were almost interchangeable as being associated with conditions that cause unhappiness. The slang verb *blighter* meant a disgraceful person or situation. In medieval times, blighters were held responsible for plagues within a household or community. In agriculture, *blight* eventually was used to describe specific **fungal** diseases of crop plants. Blights commonly caused widespread human suffering by producing famines due to excessive crop losses.

THE GREAT PLAGUES OF HUMANITY

In addition to measles, humanity has seen many plagues since ancient times. Among the most well-known account of plagues are the Egyptian Plagues mentioned in the book of Exodus in the Old Testament. These were the calamities God imposed on Egypt to convince the Pharaoh to release the Israelites from slavery. The plagues involved diseases, infestations, or hardships. Flies, frogs, lice, and locusts were the infestations. The diseases included infectious conditions such as boils, unexplained mass deaths, and livestock ailments. Fire, hail, and rivers of blood created the hardships.

Historians have identified accounts of plagues in many historical writings. The most precise chronicles of plagues are those of the **pandemic** plagues that ravaged Europe. A pandemic is a disease that spreads from one country to another and

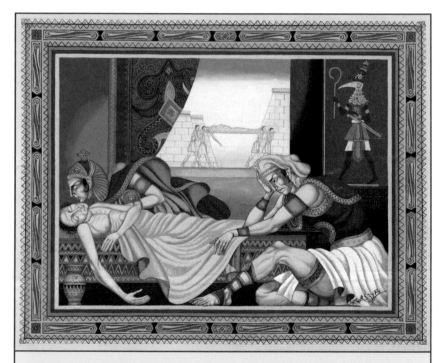

Figure 2.1 Plagues of diseases have followed humans throughout history, and people sometimes thought that displeased deities sent epidemics to punish people. This painting shows one of the plagues of Egypt from the Christian bible. (© Visual Arts Library/Art Resource, N.Y.)

across continents. **Bubonic** or **black plague** is the most famous of the pandemic plagues. Bubonic plague is a bacterial disease spread by fleas that transfer a certain form of bacteria from rats to humans. It causes internal bleeding and sores throughout the body. The first accounts of bubonic plague come from Egypt and Greece circa A.D. 540. The disease recurred across Europe between 1347 and 1889. These periodic episodes of plague devastated European populations each time they struck. Revised estimates suggest that during the height of a given outbreak, anywhere from 45 to 75 percent of the population died from black plague in many of the major European cities.

Another classic plague was a **contagious** bacterial disease called cholera. Like many contagious diseases, cholera spreads easily from food and water contaminated with the feces of people who have the disease. Attacks of cholera have occurred worldwide since 700 B.C. It still shows up commonly throughout Africa, Asia, and South America. The usually fatal disease causes serious intestinal distress and dehydration.

Smallpox is a deadly viral disease that causes severe damage to the internal organs and skin. The virus is spread by direct contact and by touching objects contaminated with the smallpox virus. It was first recorded as a major health concern in 1350 B.C. during the Egyptian and Hittite war. It reached Europe around the 1400s and was present in the United States by the 1770s. Smallpox is the only plague that has been eradicated through a worldwide vaccination effort. The last incidence of smallpox occurred in Somalia in 1977.

Poliomyelitis, or polio, is an infectious viral disease that leads to a loss of muscle function. It is spread by ingestion of material contaminated with the feces of an infected person. The disease was commonly transmitted by food handlers. Many people died when their bodies became unable to control breathing. Polio was first recorded in Egyptian writings as a disfiguring plague around 1500 B.C. The disease spread throughout the world and many people were affected until polio vaccines brought the disease under control in the twentieth century. Polio today is a very rare. However, cases regularly appear in many developing nations.

Malaria is an ancient disease that likely began afflicting animals and humans 10,000 years ago. It did not become recognized as a plague until the slave trade transported malaria to the Americas from Africa. Malaria is caused by organisms called **protists** that are spread by mosquitoes. Protists are microscopic organisms that have a **nucleus** and are generally composed of a single cell. The malaria protists are **parasites** that damage the blood cells and the liver. Malaria is still a major disease throughout tropical nations.

Yellow fever is the newest of the pandemic plagues and was likely introduced into the Americas by the African slave trade and explorations of Central and South America. The first confirmed occurrence of this viral disease took place in the 1640s in the Caribbean. It is spread by mosquitoes, causes damage throughout the body, and commonly leads to death.

Syphilis became a plague in Europe around the 1400s and was often confused with other diseases such as bubonic plague and smallpox. It is caused by bacteria that are transmitted by sexual contact. Research shows that the disease possibly originated in the Caribbean and was spread worldwide by the 1600s as world exploration and trade expanded.

Malnutrition produces ailments caused by a lack of certain nutrients in the diet, and these conditions were sometimes identified as plagues, such as beriberi, rickets, and **scurvy**. Beriberi is caused by a lack of vitamin B1, or thiamine. Rickets is a bone disease caused by inadequate vitamin D in the diet. A lack of vitamin C, or ascorbic acid, produces the disease scurvy, which is a condition that affects the skin and teeth.

Other types of infectious maladies that were not considered plagues also ravaged the world. These include influenza and many types of fevers. Diseases like leprosy, a bacterial disease that affects skin and nerves, were not highly contagious, therefore they were not categorized with the plague diseases. Leprosy was a highly feared disease because it disfigured the person and produced irregular swelling of the skin.

WHAT CAUSES A PLAGUE?

It is unlikely that prehistoric cultures suffered from many devastating plagues. Many human settlements were small and spread across large areas of the continents, limiting contact and opportunities to spread infection. In addition, many people were nomadic and moved from place to place from one generation to the next. Plagues require dense communities to gain a foothold in the population. This situation provides a means for the organisms to travel readily from person to person either directly or through a vector. A vector is an organism or object that passes a disease between people or between other organisms. Many diseases need to pass somewhat quickly from one

Figure 2.2 Cockroaches, mice, and rats can all be disease vectors for humans. The deer mouse shown here spreads the Hantavirus, which causes a severe respiratory infection. (Courtesy CDC/James Gathany)

person to the next. If they do not get into another person, the plague organism may die in the environment or may end up harming vector organisms. In addition, people who live in one area for long periods of time are more likely to remain in contact with vectors that spread disease. So, large urban areas are ideal for nurturing plague organisms.

Two well-known vectors for many human diseases are cockroaches and rats. Permanent dwellings and congested human housing becomes favorable for infestations of these pests. Agriculture appears to be another major contributing factor to the development of human plagues. Many human plagues were diseases that existed in wild animals that were domesticated for agricultural purposes. Living in proximity to the domesticated animals permitted the transmission of animal diseases to humans. DNA studies show that influenza was at one time a disease of pigs and that it became a human disease only after the domestication of pigs. Similarly, malaria started out as a cattle disease, and a childhood disease called pinkeye is common in cows. Even the fungal skin disease called ringworm originated as a fur condition in cats and dogs.

Prehistoric people did not associate plagues with infectious organisms, of which they had no knowledge. It is probable that the few plague diseases they had experienced were attributed to the perils of everyday life. Ancient Asian and Middle Eastern cultures associated plagues with living habits. They devised various types of rules and treatments to deal with the plagues. The early Greek and Roman civilizations based their medical information of plague on remedies related to cleansing of the body and the mind. Most of the enduring medical developments perfected by the Greeks and Romans emphasized the treatment of war injuries.

The European Dark Ages and the Middle Ages, which spanned approximately 476 to 1500, saw few advances in understanding the growing number of human plagues. Plagues were usually viewed as the result of moral weaknesses.

NEW PLAGUES?

It is now known that many of the old human plagues were diseases of domesticated animals. Scientists used DNA analysis studies to determine the origin of these plague bacteria and viruses. These studies were carried out by comparing the DNA of the human plague organisms to the DNA of similar organisms that cause diseases in domesticated and wild animals. DNA makes up the genetic material of almost all organisms. It provides important clues about an organism's characteristics and its relationship to other organisms.

Scientists discovered that certain changes in animal plague organisms allow them to cause diseases in humans.

Figure 2.3   These chickens were destroyed in an effort to control avian flu, a type of influenza that can infect both birds and humans. (© AP Images)

continues

continued

These new diseases of humans are called emerging diseases. Emerging diseases are becoming the new human plagues and are the subject of much news coverage. Among the most recent emerging diseases are Ebola, bird flu (avian influenza), flesh-eating staph, and West Nile virus. Global programs are underway to prevent these diseases from becoming worldwide plagues. These diseases are capable of making millions of people seriously ill in almost every nation.

Preventative medicine methods and disease treatments had strong religious foundations. Herbal remedies and treatments with toxic metals were commonly used to ward off or rid a plague from the body or from an area. Many of these medical practices were done to purify the body. It was believed that impure acts or thoughts caused the plagues. Unfortunately, most of these treatments were ineffective or caused severe harm to the people being treated. Many people treated with mercury drinks and vapors suffered dizziness, hearing loss, impaired speech, loss of coordination, muscle weakness, and vision problems.

It was during the Renaissance period in the 1600s that people started recognizing the true nature of plagues. Following the invention of the microscope, microorganisms were discovered and many scientists equated plagues to infections with these organisms. Prevention included ways to stop the organisms from being transmitted. Food and water cleanliness was practiced to reduce the spread of certain plagues such as cholera. Sanitary practices, such as proper sewage disposal, greatly reduced the spread of disease. In the 1700s, people learned to enhance the body's defenses using various medical and nutritional practices. This was reflected in the common military practice of providing sailors and troops with limes and lemons to ward off scurvy. In addition, people learned to change their environment and living conditions in order to reduce exposure to vectors. By the late 1800s, drugs were developed to kill the microorganisms that caused certain plagues. Advances in **biochemistry** and **genetics** resulted in a better understanding of the microorganisms that caused plagues. These discoveries led to better ways of preventing and treating particular plague organisms without causing significant harm to the patient or the environment.

THE MEASLES DISEASES AS A PLAGUE

Measles is a term used to describe two unrelated viral diseases called rubeola and rubella; for much of history, these diseases were viewed interchangeably or lumped together. The measles diseases were two of many human plagues that afflicted people throughout history. It was often difficult to distinguish measles from many other diseases. Many plagues were described using general terms that can be interpreted in different ways. Plagues commonly manifested as diseases that produced a fever, rash, or a sore. It is believed that the word *measles* came from the Middle Dutch word *masel* and the Middle English term *mesele*. Both of these similar words were interpreted as a blemish, or a sore on the skin. Middle Dutch and Middle English were spoken in the Netherlands and England, respectively, from around 1100 to 1500.

The original word for measles came from the Medieval Latin *misellus*, which meant "leper," or a person with leprosy. Leprosy was one of the oldest known ailments of ancient and modern times and was used as a reference point for other diseases that affect the skin. Leprosy can produce large blemishes and rashes. This in turn gave rise to a term for leprosy being used to describe measles. The fact that measles was first identified as a blemish shows that it was confused with other diseases. *Blemish* comes from the Old French term *blesmir*, which means "to turn pale after an injury." This type of naming system occurred with many of the plague diseases.

Measles was identified as being one of the plagues that produced red, circular spots on the body. Much of Europe called measles the "Red Menace" based on this early diagnosis. References to a disease resembling measles date back to at least to 2000 B.C. in the western regions of Asia. Descriptions of diseases that resembled measles appear in Greek records from 400 B.C. and African medical writings from 250 B.C.

It is now believed that measles also may have been confused with other diseases such as smallpox that were also prevalent in those regions of the world. Smallpox was a deadly infectious disease that produced red spots on the skins. The first accurate description of measles was provided by a Persian physician named Abu Bakr Muhammad ibn Zakariya Razi, who lived from 860 to 932. He published his findings in a book entitled *Kitab fi al-jadari wa-al-hasbah* ("Smallpox and Measles"), which was written in Arabic. He believed the disease was more deadly than the dreaded smallpox.

TWO KINDS OF MEASLES

American and European physicians in the 1800s began to recognize that measles referred to two different diseases. Both produced skin rashes and symptoms similar to a cold. However, one of the measles diseases was associated with a high fever and the other was accompanied by muscle aches. The high-fever measles became known as eruptive fever and later was called rubeola. Rubeola is the disease normally associated with the term measles. Rubeola describes the red color of the eruptions, or rash, on the skin. In Latin, the word *rubeus* means "red." The other disease became known after the 1880s as epidemic roseola, also known as German measles, liberty measles, and three-day measles. It was later given the scientific name rubella, meaning that it was a more mild form of measles, although it was later discovered to be a disease unique from rubeola. Physicians often use the term *German measles* for rubella because it is most well known by that name, which it got because it was first accurately described in German medical literature.

Rubeola and rubella are not the scourges that they were in the past. Modern methods of detecting and preventing viral diseases have reduced much of the public fear of measles. Before 1963, almost every child in the United States contracted rubeola and rubella. Aggressive preventative treatment programs that began in 1963 decreased the incidence of rubeola. Government strategies for reducing childhood diseases in the United States helped reduce the occurrence of rubella by 1971. Vaccinations are given as a preventive measure to reduce the spread of the disease. Today, it is unusual for children in North America and Europe to contract either rubeola or rubella. Younger physicians in these regions hardly encounter cases of either disease and usually learn to diagnose them by viewing photographs from research studies.

3
Rubeola:
The Red Measles

Red measles, commonly called "the measles," is not considered a deadly disease in developed nations with ample medical care. Adequate disease prevention programs are believed to reduce the severity of the disease. However, certain populations lack adequate medical care, meaning that red measles could be a potentially dangerous disease, particularly in children. A study conducted by the Centers for Disease Control and Prevention in 1991 compared the severity of measles in Amish populations to the severity of the disease in people living in poverty. Neither of these populations receive measles vaccinations—the Amish due to their religious convictions and the poor due to their general lack of access to medical care. The Amish people showed the same lower severity of the disease as people who were protected from measles but contracted the disease. Unprotected people living in poverty were reported to have severe cases of measles including a high incidence of brain damage caused by the virus. This study showed that living conditions are a primary factor in the dangers posed by measles.[1]

WHAT IS THE RUBEOLA VIRUS?
Contemporary biologists, such as Jared Diamond, are aware that the rubeola virus at one time did not cause disease in humans. He writes in the book *Guns, Germs and Steel* that "Measles and TB [tuberculosis] evolved from diseases of our cattle, influenza from a disease of pigs, and smallpox possibly from a disease of camels. The Americas had very few native domesticated animal species from which humans could acquire such diseases."[2]

Rubeola is an emerging disease virus that at one time affected only domesticated animals. Rubeola likely developed from a cattle disease called rinderpest. Viruses usually only infect one particular type of organism. This is because of the way that the virus must enter the organism's cells. The virus needs to bind to a specific cell surface protein that promotes entry of the virus into the cell. These proteins are unique for each organism. The original rubeola virus, like with other viral emergent diseases, underwent a genetic change called a **mutation** that altered the virus's ability to enter cattle cells. By chance, these mutations can enable the virus to attach to another organism's cells. This then produces a new type of virus that invades a different kind of organism and creates an emerging disease. Over the course of civilization, humans have

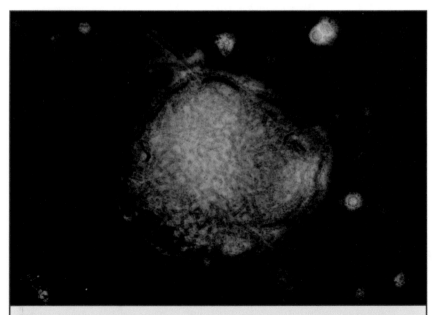

Figure 3.1 This is a color transmission electron micrograph of the rubeola virus (red measles). This virus is believed to have mutated from a virus that infects cows into a virus that infects people. (© CDC/Photo Researchers, Inc.)

remained in close enough contact with cattle to pick up several emerging diseases.

The rubeola virus belongs to the **genus *Morbillivirus*.** *Morbillivirus* causes a variety of **distemper** and measles diseases in cattle, dogs, dolphins, porpoises, and seals. *Morbillivirus* and related viruses are categorized in a larger group called the **Paramyxoviridae.** The Paramyxoviridae group of viruses infects mostly birds and mammals. They cause a variety of diseases specific to a particular animal. Some viruses can pass between two different organisms, causing similar diseases. For example, avian influenza virus primarily infects birds, but can also cause disease in humans.

The rubeola virus possesses an envelope that can have a variety of shapes. It is not fully known why the viral envelope varies—it likely has to do with the way the viral capsid forms and how it exits the host cell. Many are spherical and others are **filamentous,** or ropelike in shape. The spherical forms are no larger than 0.00025 millimeters in diameter. This means that more than 100,000 viruses put side by side would be less than one inch (2.54 cm). Filamentous rubeola viruses can be as

CATEGORIZING VIRUSES

Scientists who research viruses do not usually use names when referring to a particular virus. They use a system of codes to categorize the virus. The latest method of categorizing viruses by a code is the International Committee on Taxonomy of Viruses system. For example, the human measles virus is assigned Virus Code 48.1.2.0.001. The numbers 48.1.2.0 refers to the *Morbillivirus* genus and 48 includes all of the Paramyxoviridae viruses. Older coding systems placed the viruses into numbered groups based on the characteristics of their genome and capsid. Subcategories were determined by the type of host infected by the virus.

large as 0.01 millimeters long. Projecting from the envelope are protein spikes. These spikes are called **hemagglutinins** because they cause **red blood cells** to clump upon sticking to the virus. This clumping can cause body damage by blocking blood flow to important organs.

Within the envelope is a nucleocapsid that tightly protects the genome. The nucleocapsid is filamentous and is twisted into a type of spiral called a **helix**. The diameter of the helix determines the characteristics of the envelope. It is slightly smaller than the envelope, measuring 0.00018 millimeters in diameter. As the virus buds from the host, the envelope closely surrounds the outer surface of the nucleocapsid. As a result, the envelope takes on the approximate shape of the nucleocapsid. The twisting of the helix varies, thereby producing different shapes to the virus.

The rubeola genome is a single strand of RNA. Interestingly, this RNA strand can be a positive strand or a negative strand. However, there are usually more negative-strand viruses produced in the host. Negative-strand viruses must be converted to positive-strand viruses before they can replicate; positive-strand viruses are able to seize control of a cell and begin replicating immediately.

The difference in strand type is likely due to variability in the way the genome is packaged in the nucleocapsid. As the cell replicates the virus, negative-strand RNA is used to make copies of the positive strand. In turn, positive-strand copies are used to control the cell and to make negative strands. This leaves a mixture of negative and positive strands. Most viruses are not very precise in the way they build nucleocapsids. So the nucleocapsid in rubeola viruses readily packages either type of strand. However, the proteins of nucleocapsid are likely better designed to package negative strands.

A virus's genome is measured in size by the number of nucleic acids making up its genome. Each nucleic acid is also called a base pair. Genome size is typically represented with the symbol *nt* for **nucleotide**. Humans have a genome that is 3 billion nt. *Paramyxovirus* genomes are 17,000 to 20,000 nt. Rubeola has an intermediate-sized genome, containing 15,900 nt. The rubeola genome is composed of six **genes** separated by repeated sequences of nucleic acids that have no particular role. These repeated sequences are very likely areas along the genome that space apart the genes. The genome also contains a starting region at the beginning of the genome and an ending region at the other side. These starting and ending regions guide the cell to make the viral proteins in the correct sequence.

Rubeola infects a cell by first fusing to the cell membrane. It then enters the cell's **cytoplasm**, where it is uncoated. The negative-strand RNA is converted into a positive-strand RNA. This positive strand then directs the cell to produce nucleocapsids and negative strands. The strands are then packaged in the nucleocapsids, which exit the cell by budding. A large amount of empty nucleocapsids are produced in the infected host cells. This produces characteristic objects called **inclusion bodies** in the cytoplasm of cells infected with rubeola and related viruses. Rubeola viruses have envelope proteins that cause adjacent host cells to fuse with each other. This fused condition is called a **syncytium** and is easily seen with a microscope. The syncytium disrupts cell function and contributes to some of the illness associated with the infection.

WHAT IS THE RUBEOLA DISEASE?

Early in history, rubeola was often confused with other diseases. People at the time categorized rubeola as one of the many plagues that produced red blotches on the skin. Very little attention was given to the other ailments associated with rubeola that made it distinguishable from the other plagues. The earliest recorded medical description of rubeola was made around 900 by Persian physician Abu Bakr Muhammad ibn Zakariya Razi. Razi believed that measles and smallpox were two forms of the same disease. However, he kept detailed notes so that physicians were able to tell with some accuracy a pure case of measles from a smallpox infection.

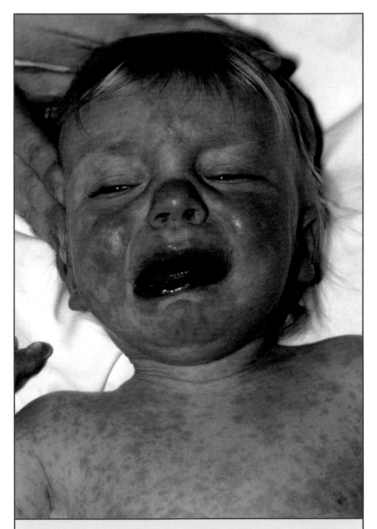

Figure 3.2 A distinctive skin rash is the classic sign of rubeola. The rash and other signs and symptoms of rubeola begin to appear one to two weeks after exposure. (© Dr. M.A. Ansary/Photo Researchers, Inc.)

Unfortunately, most people in early history contracted measles with other diseases, such as smallpox. So it was not possible to tell if a particular ailment was due to measles or to another disease. It was not until the 1500s in Europe that other diseases became less common and measles was more readily recognized based on Razi's description. Today physicians are able to quickly recognize measles and have detailed journals of disease conditions associated with the virus. However, even a pure measles infection can produce a diversity of conditions based on the person's age, ethnicity, gender, and general health.

The illnesses produced by measles and other diseases are categorized as signs and symptoms. A sign is any evidence of the presence of a disorder or disease that can be measured or detected. Detection can involve visual examination using the eyes or a microscope. Signs can be detected with medical instruments. Examples of signs include blisters, a fever, a sore throat, and vomiting. A symptom is any evidence of a disease as perceived by the patient. Symptoms cannot be measured or detected by the physician or by medical instrumentation. Pain and nausea are symptoms.

Rubeola does not cause signs and symptoms upon contamination. A virus causes disease only after it starts replicating within the cells it infects. The period between contamination and the presentation of signs or symptoms is called the incubation period. The **incubation period** varies greatly among infectious diseases. Much of this variation is due to the type of organism causing the infection. Each type of infectious organism has a particular rate of replication. Also, the time it takes for the organism to become established in the body contributes to the incubation period. Certain infectious organisms take longer to get the resources they need for survival and replication.

The incubation period for rubeola ranges from 7 to 14 days after exposure to the virus. This is much longer than the incubation period of a cold virus, which averages two to four days, and shorter than the chicken pox virus, which is 14 to 16 days. Within this incubation period, the rubeola virus accomplishes several tasks. First, it is transported to host cells by a variety of means. Often rubeola virus is transported by fluids and **mucus** on the contaminated body surfaces. Mucus is a slimy material produced by certain cells lining the digestive system, the respiratory system, and the **urogenital system**. Rubeola is capable of entering the cells of the skin and these other body systems.

Rubeola usually enters the body through the mouth and nose. It then enters the **epithelial cells** that line the upper part of the respiratory system. Upon entering the epithelial cells, the virus begins its replication process. The viruses spread from cell to cell and this in turn carries the infection down the respiratory system. Fortunately, the body is aware of the viral infection at this early point of the disease. Chemicals called **interleukins** are released by the infected cells early during the infection. Interleukins are chemicals that protect the body from viral infections. In response to the interleukins, blood cells release chemicals called **interferons** that reduce the ability of the viruses to infect cells. A full immune response begins as the number of viruses in the body increases because the immune system is getting more of the interleukin signals. This response produces the signs and symptoms that are typical of rubeola infection.

SIGNS AND SYMPTOMS OF RUBEOLA

Rubeola is probably most recognized for the flat red rash that it causes on all surfaces of the skin. Physicians call it a **diffuse macular** rash. The rash normally has a red or reddish-brown spotted appearance. It is typical for the rash to show up on the forehead. It then spreads over the face and neck. Eventually the whole body, including the hands and feet, is covered with the rash. Small red spots with bluish centers—called **Koplik's spots**—appear in the mouth. The rash and Koplik's spots are both actually an **allergy** to immune system chemicals produced to fight off the virus.

A rash and Koplik's spots are not usually the first signs of rubeola. Other signs and symptoms that appear first can be confused with other diseases, which may make it difficult for physicians to initially identify the condition. Rubeola most commonly enters the body through the upper respiratory system, irritating the cells lining the upper respiratory system. This causes one of the first signs of the disease: a hacking cough. The irritation and cough usually brings about an immune response that produces the next series of signs and symptoms. Chemicals called **histamines** produce a runny nose and watery eyes. The

SICK AND TIRED

Many diseases, including rubeola, cause the body to produce histamines, which are chemicals made by immune system cells during an immune response. This is one of the body's first defenses against infection and injury. Histamines facilitate what is called the inflammatory response: swelling, redness, pain, and heat. Sometimes the inflammatory response goes too far and accidentally harms the body. Physicians sometimes give a patient drugs called antihistamines that reduce the inflammation. They give a large enough dose to relieve the swelling and pain without inhibiting the body's defenses against diseases.

Unfortunately, antihistamines have consequences because they cause most people to become drowsy and sluggish. In the past, people needing to stay alert and awake have had to avoid antihistamines for this reason. Researchers have since learned that various types of cells respond to histamines in different ways. Scientists who develop medicines were able to formulate specialized antihistamines that can slow down specific features of inflammation without affecting the overall response. This made it possible to administer antihistamine treatments that do not cause drowsiness and sluggishness.

body produces histamines as an alert about damage or disease. They stimulate other blood cells and immune system cells to carry out the steps needed to fight disease and repair body damage. Again, it is difficult to suspect rubeola as the cause of these signs because coughing, runny nose, and watery eyes are associated with many diseases. Itchy skin is the symptom that follows the runny nose and watery eyes. This also is caused by the histamines. It is at this point that the rash and Koplik's spots begin to appear.

Interleukins that are produced to fight off the virus also induce a fever. Specific types of interleukins and other immune system chemicals can be **pyrogens**, substances that cause fever. At first the fever is mild, but then may reach 104°F, or 40°C. The fever is most noticeable after the spots appear. With the fever comes a general feeling of discomfort and tiredness. Symptoms at this point can also include a headache and nausea. Many people with rubeola complain about sensitivity to light and have trouble keeping their eyes open in bright room light or outdoors. Light sensitivity is usually accompanied by red and irritated eyes.

Most cases of rubeola usually last for three to five days until the fever goes away. However, it may take a few more days for all of the other signs and symptoms to disappear. During the recovery process, the red rash starts to turn a brownish color, and the top layers of skin peel off. This removes all evidence of the rash. The Koplik's spots gradually fade away and leave the lining of the mouth looking normal with no scarring.

In some people, rubeola can spread beyond the respiratory system to produce infections in other body parts. This is rare and usually happens in people with weakened immune responses. Inadequate diets, severe stress, and infections by other disease organisms can reduce the immune system's ability to fight off the rubeola virus. Rubeola can spread to the digestive system and cause an infection of the appendix. In some children rubeola can invade cells leading up to the middle part of the ear. This is usually accompanied by discomfort and pain at the base of the neck below the ears. Nausea can also be a symptom of ear infection if balance is affected.

In rare cases, the measles virus can spread to the brain, causing **encephalitis**. Encephalitis is any disease that causes damage and swelling of the brain. This condition can have different degrees of severity. The most dangerous form of encephalitis occurs when rubeola permanently remains in the brain. This produces a condition called **subacute sclerosing panencephalitis (SSPE),** which is defined as progressive damage to the brain that is usually caused by viral infections. SSPE may not appear until years after the initial rubeola infection. In many cases this condition leads to death. The rubeola virus does not normally cause brain damage. However, certain forms of the virus are able to invade the brain. Unfortunately, it is difficult for physicians to identify the form of rubeola causing an infection.

Other diseases may invade the body during a rubeola infection because the body's immune system is already under stress. This makes it difficult for the body to fight off other infections. This adds to the complexity of signs and symptoms. Plus, these additional diseases can cause their own severe complications that may result in death. Irritation of the respiratory system by rubeola can encourage the growth of bacteria in the ears and lungs. The most common type of secondary infection is pneumonia. Pneumonia produces a severe cough that lasts for more than five days. Yellow or green mucus is also evident during coughing. The color comes from bacterial growth and immune system cells in the mucus. Bacteria can also invade the inner and middle parts of the ear during a rubella infection. This produces an ear infection called **otitis media**. People who are naturally susceptible to bacterial infections are likely to develop dangerous conditions that add complications to the rubeola infection.

For most people, however, rubeola is a mild disease that runs its course with no long-term health effects. The body usually combats the virus and is able to clear up the signs and symptoms within a week after the incubation period. People with weakened immune systems take longer to recover from the disease. They are likely to suffer from more tissue damage because the virus is able to spread more readily throughout the body. Bacteria are also likely to invade and damage the lungs in people with a deficient immune system.

4

Rubella:
The German Measles

In 2002, W. Robert Lee and Peter Marschalck of the University of Liverpool in England evaluated old medical data to come up with new conclusions about infant death. They were investigating the probable factors that reduce the chances of infant deaths. Previously unpublished medical records showed a steady decline of infant deaths in both rural and urban German communities from 1750 to 1850. They discovered that during that time period a rising standard of living and improvements in preventative care decreased the severity of diseases that kill infants. The decline in German measles was a major factor in reducing infant death.[1]

WHAT IS THE RUBELLA VIRUS?
Throughout much of human history, disease was viewed as a sign of physical or moral weakness. Accordingly, any treatments reflected this attitude and provided little cure. Today it is widely known that German measles, or rubella, is a preventable viral disease that is spread from person to person by casual contact.

Unlike rubeola, rubella is truly a human disease that may have been present throughout humanity's existence. Rubella is not found in any other animals. Rubella is the only representative of its virus category, belonging to the genus ***Rubivirus***. Rubella is the only member of this genus, which exclusively causes disease in humans. *Rubivirus* belongs to a larger category of viruses called the **Togaviridae**.

Most togaviruses infect insects and mammals. Insects usually transmit the viruses to mammals through bites. These viruses normally live in the salivary glands of mosquitoes. The virus travels through the bloodstream of mammals to invade many organs including the brain and skin. Togaviruses belong to a group of viruses called the **arboviruses**. Arboviruses are a large of group of viruses spread by insects to animals and plants. They cause a variety of human diseases that can produce ailments such as bleeding, brain damage, diarrhea, fever, and organ damage. Arboviruses can spread from birds to domestic animals to humans. Currently, arborvirus diseases are becoming more common worldwide. As a result, there are now rigorous programs to control biting insects that spread the diseases.

Togaviruses, such as *Rubivirus*, are characterized by their rapid replication rate. Upon entering the body, the

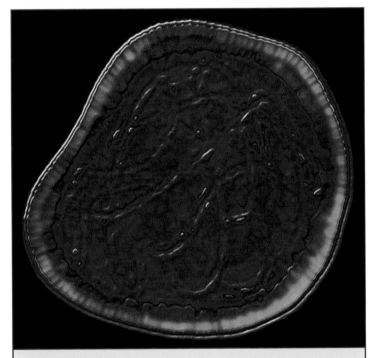

Figure 4.1 This is a color transmission micrograph of a rubella virus (German measles). Unlike rubeola, rubella is found only in humans. (© Alfred Pasieka/Photo Researchers, Inc.)

virus makes its way to various organs by being transported in bodily fluids and the bloodstream. It enters the cells by attaching to the cell surface using the protein spikes on the envelope. The envelope blends with the cell surface, releasing the virus capsid and genome inside the cell fluids. Unfortunately, little is known about how the virus actually enters the cell. This lack of knowledge makes it difficult to develop drugs that control rubella.

Rubivirus has a spherical envelope that ranges in size from 0.000065 to 0.00007 millimeters in diameter. It is almost one-third the size of rubeola virus. The surface of the envelope is covered with 80 protein spikes that help the virus attach to and enter host cells. *Rubivirus* has an angular capsid made up of 240 identical protein parts. Inside the capsid is the single-stranded RNA genome, which is very small and only composed of approximately 12,000 bits of genetic information (compared to the six billion found in humans). This genome is similar to molecules naturally found in the cell that program for proteins. This similarity may protect the virus after it enters the host cell. The cell likely avoids destroying the virus because the viral genome blends in with the cell's chemistry.

Once inside the cell, the capsid proteins fall apart, exposing the genome. The genome then uses the cell's chemistry to produce many new viral capsids and genomes. *Rubivirus* has a positive-strand RNA genome, meaning that unlike the rubeola virus it is immediately able to replicate upon entering a cell. A complete virus is formed when the genome is packaged in a capsid. Little is known about the rubella viral assembly stages. Its small capsid makes the virus very difficult to study even using the most powerful magnification tools. After the assembly stage, the virus buds out of the cell. The budding process covers the capsid with the envelope. These mature viruses are now ready to spread throughout the body to rapidly invade other cells. Many of the viruses can also exit the body through bodily fluids such as saliva.

Replication of the rubella virus causes damage to **mitochondria**, which are critical components of cells. Mitochondria are structures within a cell responsible for the conversion of food into cell energy. Consequently, the virus interferes with a cell's ability to produce energy to run living processes. This impairs the cell and can even lead to cell death after a certain level of viral infection.

WHAT IS THE RUBELLA DISEASE?

Rubella, like rubeola and many diseases of ancient times, was often confused with other diseases called plagues and poxes. The earliest mention of measles was by the Greek physician Thucydides, who described a plague of Athens in 430 B.C. However, it is believed he confused rubella with a bacterial disease called typhoid. By the tenth century, Persian physicians were able to distinguish the measles diseases from smallpox. The severe form of measles, now known to be German measles, was considered worse than smallpox.

Medical records from the 1400s indicate that what was likely German measles was prevalent throughout Asia, Europe, and the Middle East. It was most prevalent in large, crowded cities. The most accurate descriptions of German measles were recorded in the 1500s and 1600s. German physician Friedrich Hoffmann made the first clinical description of rubella in 1740. His findings were confirmed by many other European physicians in the 1700s and 1800s. By the early 1800s, rubella was no longer confused with other diseases or allergies.

Rubella typically enters the body by attaching to epithelial cells lining the mouth and nose. They then infect these cells, releasing new viruses into the surrounding tissues. The virus can then travel down the upper part of the respiratory system. Some viruses enter the bloodstream by passing through the numerous blood vessels in the respiratory system. The viruses begin to replicate in the first cells they encounter, then spread to cells throughout the body. They infect nearby cells and cells that

Figure 4.2   Friedrich Hoffmann. (Courtesy National Library of Medicine/ U.S. National Institutes of Health)

they encounter when they are transported by the blood flow. Interleukins are then produced by the infected cells. Other cells slow down viral replication as a response to the interleukins traveling in the body fluids and blood. The infection becomes evident as more and more interleukins are released.

The virus requires incubation time of two to three weeks between entering the body and the appearance of signs and symptoms. After entering the body, rubella enters and multiplies in the cells that line the nose and throat. However, it is possible for rubella to enter the bloodstream, giving it access to every body organ. It enters the blood through small blood vessels in the lining of the respiratory system. From there, the virus is capable of replicating in the brain, eyes, joints, lungs, **lymph nodes**, spleen, testes, and tonsils.

The rubella virus passes from one person to another through fluids from the nose and throat. It is easily passed along when an infected person coughs or sneezes on other people. Children especially can transfer the virus from hands contaminated with mucus and saliva. Rubella is easily spread one week before to one week after the incubation period. Infected people can spread the virus even if no signs and symptoms are evident.

SIGNS AND SYMPTOMS OF RUBELLA

Many physicians are frustrated by possible cases of rubella. It is very difficult to diagnose the disease in the early stages after infection because the signs and symptoms are frequently very mild and resemble the early stages of many bacterial and viral infections. It can often be confused with common colds and influenza. Rubella becomes distinguishable from other diseases two to three weeks after exposure to the virus. It is usually more difficult to tell in young children, because it resembles many other diseases. The signs and symptoms normally last about two to three days after the initial appearance of disease. This is why rubella is often called three-day measles. It does not persist as long as rubeola, which can last for two weeks.

The signs and symptoms of rubella vary with the person's age and overall health. It is often more severe in people with a weakened immune system. Malnutrition, substance abuse, and stress suppress the immune system, making it more favorable for the virus to spread and replicate. People with AIDS are very susceptible to dangerous rubella infections. This is also true for cancer patients being treated with **chemotherapy**. The first signs of rubella are normally a stuffy or runny nose typical of colds. It then progresses to general feelings of **malaise**, a low-grade fever, and diarrhea. The fever runs 99°F to 100°F and causes only mild discomfort. It rarely elevates above 102°F. These signs and symptoms typically last one to five days.

As rubella spreads down the respiratory system, it produces a headache and possibly reddening in the back of the throat. The lymph nodes in the neck may also become swollen. It usually affects the lymph nodes at the base of the skull, the back of the neck, and behind the ears. Lymph node enlargement results from the immune system attacking the viral infection. The lymph nodes store cells involved in producing antibodies and other chemicals that defend against the virus.

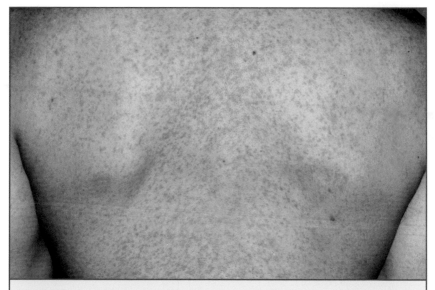

Figure 4.3 Rubella causes a pinkish rash. The signs and symptoms of rubella become distinguishable from those of other diseases two to three weeks after exposure. (© Pulse Picture Library/CMP Images/Phototake)

Tonsils, which are lymph nodes of the throat, are generally affected and can swell substantially. This may make it painful to swallow. Some people show reddened eyes and inflammation of the **conjunctiva**, which is a thin, skin-like layer covering the front surface of the eye.

A small, pink rash begins to develop on the face about three days after the first signs of infection. Physicians describe the rash as **maculopapular**, meaning that there are both flat and raised spots. The rash quickly spreads to the trunk, and in many people it also shows up on arms and legs. This rash is usually composed of a large number of fine red spots. The spots are usually uniformly distributed on the affected body parts. In some cases it may be patchy and unevenly dispersed. Unlike rubeola, the rubella rash is not bright red and distinctively patchy. Severe cases of rubella can resemble rubeola rashes in the early stages of the disease.

The rubella rash varies in intensity and in distribution from person to person. Itchiness is usually associated with the rash. However, the intensity of the rash does not predict the amount of itchiness. Itching is due to the release of histamines by **white blood cells** reacting to the viral infection. People must be careful when scratching the sores. The rashes can be scratched open, potentially letting bacteria enter the body through the open sores and cause a secondary infection. The rash usually disappears after three days in the same sequence that it appeared.

In older children and adults, rubella may be accompanied by soreness and inflammation in their joints. Again, this is caused by histamines flowing in the blood that is then deposited in different tissues. Children and young adults may experience a loss of appetite as is typical with many illnesses. Luckily for most people, the rubella virus does not have any long-term effects on the body. The disease causes no permanent damage, unlike other common diseases of childhood such as chicken pox. However, other infections that can invade the body during a bout of rubella can cause significant problems. Rubella is not categorized as a typically deadly disease except in children who are in extremely poor health.

CONGENITAL RUBELLA

There is one important exception to the generally harmless effects of rubella. If a pregnant woman contracts rubella, it can have long-lasting effects on her developing fetus, a condition called **congenital rubella syndrome**. Rubella passes from the mother's blood through the **umbilical cord** and into the **placenta**. The umbilical cord contains blood vessels that permit the placenta to exchange nutrients and gases with the fetus. Unfortunately, the placenta can pass certain bacteria and viruses to the fetus. Once in the fetus, the rubella virus spreads to all the body organs. It then causes cell death, or **apoptosis**, in the rapidly growing organs of the fetus. The virus is especially dangerous to the fetus during the mother's first three months of pregnancy. Major body organs are developing during this period and any damage to these structures will produce severe damage to the body.

Physicians call congenital rubella a **teratogenic** virus in the fetus. A **teratogen** is anything capable of producing birth defects. Rubella causes birth defects by killing cells in critical organs during fetal development. The fetus's small and unformed organs are more easily damaged than adult organs. In severe cases, rubella can cause the death of the fetus. Depending on the age of the fetus, the virus is more likely to cause birth defects that can range from mild to severe. Mothers who contract rubella within the first three months of pregnancy are more likely to have fetuses with severe nervous system defects such as brain damage and deafness. Fetuses developing in the later stages of pregnancy are less likely to show significant damage. Pregnant women with weakened immune systems are more likely to pass a greater number of viruses through the placenta. This in turn can cause more damage to the fetus.

NATURE VERSUS NURTURE

On October 2, 2007, About.com columnist Jamie Berke received a surprising question about deafness. The person asking the question wrote, "My cousin is having a baby with a man that is deaf. His deafness was a result of his mother having Germany Measels [sic] when she was pregnant with him. Could their child now have a chance of being deaf also?" This question affected Berke personally because she was born profoundly deaf from congenital rubella. Her answer was simple and cautious. She replied, "As far as I know, deafness from German Measles (also known as rubella) is not hereditary."[2]

The conditions caused by congenital rubella can only be passed along by viral contamination. Rubella does not do its damage by altering the DNA in the body cells. People showing damage from rubella have normal DNA. Therefore, they are likely to produce a normal child as anybody else. Many people believe that all congenital conditions are brought about by some type of genetic damage. The contrary is most likely true. Many congenital birth defects are associated with accidental abnormalities of cell division. Birth defects can also be caused by certain hazardous chemicals, teratogenic drugs, and a variety of infectious diseases.

Congenital rubella is mainly characterized by heart and nervous system issues. Heart defects range from mild to severe. Fetuses affected early in pregnancy can develop a condition called **cardiovascular** rubella syndrome. The **syndrome** is known to cause defects to the heart valves that interfere with distribution of blood through the lungs and other body organs. Holes can also form inside the walls of heart, also leading to diminished blood flow. The inner heart walls help separate the blood-exchanging gases with the lungs from the blood vessels that transport blood throughout the body. In some cases surgery must be done so blood can flow normally through the heart. The syndrome can also produce internal bleeding in the fetus.

The ears and eyes are the most often affected organs in congenital rubella, which often causes deafness and blindness. Although hearing aids permit some degree of hearing in milder forms of ear damage, the deafness produced by rubella is generally not correctable. The child can also be born with **cataracts** in the eyes. Cataracts cause clouding of the lens of the eye, making vision very blurry. This is a mild form of blindness that can usually be corrected with surgery or glasses. In other mild cases of blindness the child has the inability to see at night or under low lighting. Other forms of blindness from rubella can also result from damage to the visual cells of the eye. This condition is called **retinal** degeneration. This type of blindness cannot be corrected. Sometimes it produces complete visual loss.

Rubella damage to the brain can produce **cerebral palsy** or mental retardation. Cerebral palsy can be caused by viral damage to the blood vessels or nerves of the brain. The condition can affect the limbs or the whole body. Mental retardation causes below-average intellectual functioning. It results from damage to nerves involved in processing and understanding information. Viral damage throughout the body organs can cause an overall slowing of development called growth retardation. Affected children are usually born smaller with organs that function less effectively. Skins lesions are also possible. Some babies are born with an enlarged liver and spleen due to injury caused by the virus and by immune system attack. It is possible for rubella to cause fetal death before birth or just after delivery of the baby.

5

Epidemiology

In 2000, The National Disease Surveillance Centre (NDSC) in Ireland reported 1,221 cases of rubeola by August of that year. Normally only 73 cases are reported per year. More than 80 percent of the cases occurred in the eastern regions of Ireland.[1] The cause of this incredible outbreak stumped public health officials. It was discovered the next year that the outbreak was due to people being afraid of measles vaccination injections. People felt that the vaccine would cause children to develop mental disorders such as autism. This was based on rumors from the United States that the conditions were linked to the vaccine. The Irish public's fear of the potential danger of the vaccine far outweighed in their minds the benefits of preventing measles. Officials from the NDSC had to implement a public education campaign to reverse the effect of the misinformation. The Irish government is now more vigilant in keeping the public informed about the necessity of vaccines for safely controlling the spread of potentially dangerous diseases.

EPIDEMIOLOGY OF INFECTIOUS DISEASES

Epidemiologists Roy M. Andersen and Robert May echoed a revealing comment about the study of infectious diseases in a book entitled *Infectious Diseases of Humans: Dynamics and Control*. They quoted science fiction writer Poul Anderson, who wrote, "I have yet to see any problem, however complicated, which, when you look at it in the right way, did not become still more complicated."[2] **Epidemiology** is the study of the occurrence and frequency of disease in populations. It entails a variety of strategies that give insight into the spread and distribution of infectious diseases. Anderson was describing the sometimes convoluted pursuit of tracking the spread of diseases such as rubella and rubeola. It may take many years to fully understand enough about an infectious disease to predict when and where it will strike in a population. Many cases of the disease must be studied over a long period of time before enough information can be collected to fully predict when a disease is likely to occur.

Epidemiology became a formal science in the late 1800s after scientists discovered the different types of organisms that cause infectious diseases. This science was born from advances in microbiology. Scientists such as Robert Koch and Louis Pasteur in the 1850s supported the view that microscopic organisms caused infectious diseases. This view became known as Germ Theory. Their views countered earlier notions that diseases were caused by filth or a lack of virtue, or by spontaneous generation, which is the belief that life could arise from nonliving materials. It took many years of compelling evidence to convince society that "unseen" organisms caused many devastating diseases. Pasteur formalized a fundamental principle of biology called **biogenesis**. Biogenesis supports the concepts that life comes from preexisting life and that infectious diseases are caused by living things.

Physicians and scientists in the late 1800s found it imperative to control deadly diseases such as polio, smallpox, and typhoid. So they started finding ways to track the spread of organisms that caused infectious diseases in humans. They also relied on the research of Robert Koch, who laid down the strategy for identifying the causative agents of infectious diseases. He proposed four criteria, or postulates, for confirming if a particular organism was the cause of an infectious disease. Koch's Postulates were: 1) the organism must be associated in every instance of the disease, 2) the organism must be extracted from the body and grown in a culture for several generations, 3) the disease could be reproduced in experimental animals through a pure culture, and 4) the organism could be retrieved from the inoculated animal and cultured again. Unfortunately, criteria 3 and 4 are not always easy to achieve. Some organisms, such as

Figure 5.1 Robert Koch, whose postulates helped set forth the criteria for identifying the causes of different diseases. (Courtesy National Library of Medicine/U.S. National Institutes of Health)

viruses, are very difficult to grow outside of a host's body. So different standards unique to growing viruses were developed for investigating viral diseases based on Koch's Postulates.

Epidemiological studies ultimately expanded to the investigation of other types of diseases. It grew to include studies of the circumstances leading to cancer, congenital disorders, diabetes, heart diseases, and high blood pressure. Many epidemiological studies today focus on the inheritance of genetic disorders. Other epidemiological studies investigate whether certain types of pollutants cause disease or make people susceptible to other types of disease. Scientists have learned that other factors that affect health make people more likely to suffer from more severe outcomes of infectious diseases. In overcrowded, impoverished areas, rubeola and rubella are more likely to spread in people who are malnourished and undernourished. Improper nutrition and the stresses of overcrowding reduce immune system function, thus increasing the likelihood that a person exposed to a disease organism will develop an infection.

Epidemiological research is carried out in two ways. One method investigates the occurrence of a disease after it has already happened. This is called **retrospective epidemiology**. Another strategy is called **prospective epidemiology** and is used to determine whether a disease may happen in a person or a population in the future. Prospective epidemiology is more accurate when it is based on many retrospective epidemiological studies. The most common form of study uses retrospective methods, particularly for new types of diseases. These studies help scientists collect comprehensive data about the causes of the occurrence of a disease. The type of data that is collected includes factors that may predispose a person to a disease, such as age, ethnicity, gender, overall health, personal habits, and socioeconomic status. A retrospective study on a new disease or a disease in an unexpected population of people is called a **case-control study**.

Epidemiologists require large amounts of detailed medical data to collect retrospective information. They gather this information from historical accounts of a disease and from current medical records. In many parts of the world, physicians are asked to report the occurrences of diseases to the Centers for Disease Control and Prevention (CDC) or the World Health Organization (WHO). The CDC is a federal organization in the United States that monitors diseases. Global diseases are studied by the WHO, which is a branch of the United Nations that monitors diseases. The information for a particular disease is statistically analyzed to determine the common conditions and causes associated with the disease. This information in turn is used to predict situations in which the disease can occur.

Epidemiologists have many terms that are important for understanding the monitoring of rubella and rubeola. **Risk factor** is a term that explains the circumstances that cause a person to develop a disease. A risk factor can be due to some attribute of the person that makes them more susceptible to a disease, such as obesity, malnutrition, or smoking. **Exposure** is a risk factor in the environment, such as a thing or a situation, that brings the organism in contact with a person. **Etiologic population** is the proportion of all disease cases that are associated with an exposure or risk. The time between the measurable onset of disease and detection of the diseases is called the **latent period. Morbidity** is used to describe any illness that results from a disease. **Mortality** is a measure of the occurrence of death from a disease in a particular population during a particular period of time.

Other important terms refer to the way a disease spreads through a population. A **carrier** is a person or animal that does not show signs of the disease but possesses the infectious agent. Carriers can unknowingly spread disease to other people. People in the early stages of mild rubeola and rubella are capable of spreading the disease through their saliva. Contagious is a term that describes a disease that can be easily transmitted from one person to another by contact or close proximity. **Endemic** describes the regular presence of a disease or infectious agent in a certain population of people. The term **epidemic** is used to explain the occurrence of more cases of disease than expected in a given area or among a specific group of people within a certain period of time.

EPIDEMIOLOGY OF RUBEOLA

Rubeola is considered a contagious disease because it is easily spread from one person to another. Many physicians consider it one of the most contagious diseases, with a high degree of morbidity. Fortunately, it has a low mortality. The rubeola virus is most commonly spread through the air. This is called airborne transmission. Airborne viruses are transferred from person to person through coughing and sneezing. Inactive virus particles travel in mucus and saliva and can infect another person when the virus enters their nose or mouth. Rubeola is most infectious this way when people are in close proximity. This type of transmission is frequent in households and schools. An infected person can spread the disease before they show the signs of rubeola. They remain contagious for about four days after the appearance of the rash.

Rubeola can also be transmitted by direct contact with contaminated nose and throat fluids. This most frequently occurs in children. Children normally transmit the virus when their hands are contaminated with mucus and saliva. The virus is spread to others through casual touching and playing. Contaminated mucus and saliva can also be transferred to objects such as toys and utensils. This is called indirect transmission or **vector-assisted transmission**. Vectors are objects or organisms that spread disease. Nonliving vectors such as utensils or surfaces are called **fomites**. Other people pick up the virus when they contact the contaminated mucus and saliva on the fomite. The rubeola virus, like many other enveloped viruses, does not survive long outside of the body. It decays within hours when exposed to air. Rubeola is likely to die more quickly in humid conditions. It is believed that moisture softens the envelope, helping it to break down more quickly.

When monitoring measles, epidemiologists define an outbreak as a group of three or more cases occurring in a small location. The small location can be a city, day care center, household, neighborhood, or school. A large outbreak can involve 15 people. A sudden increase in outbreaks sometimes occurs in a continent or a country. This then becomes an epidemic. Rubeola is called a notifiable disease because doctors must report any cases they diagnose to the CDC and the WHO. They use the information to track and avert possible epidemics.

DISEASE AMONG THE NATIVE AMERICANS

It is estimated that 18 million Native Americans lived in various tribes spread across North America before European settlement in the 1500s. The Native American population declined rapidly after their initial contact with Europeans. This population loss was at one time attributed to war and a loss of resources to maintain their population. However, researchers now have compelling evidence that a major contributing factor to this population decline was infectious disease. Early medical records show that between the sixteenth and twentieth centuries, 93 infectious disease outbreaks significantly affected Native American people. All of these were diseases carried by the European settlers. The Native Americans had not previously been exposed to these diseases and thus had no immune system protection from them so they readily became ill or died. Both types of measles were among the group of at least 15 diseases brought to the continent. Bubonic plague and smallpox were the most deadly of the diseases. It is believed from 1830s public health records that 90 percent of the original Native American population died from diseases introduced by the European settlers.[3]

Early European settlers to the Americas dealt with many measles epidemics. They brought the disease with them and introduced measles to Native American populations when they made contact with them. Frequent measles outbreaks were documented from 1657 through 1740 in Boston. Outbreaks occurred throughout the colonial settlements in the mid-1700s. New York and Philadelphia had an outbreak in 1788. Measles occurrences in the United States remained small until the late twentieth century.

The United States had a major measles epidemic from 1989 to 1991. Major urban areas such as Chicago, Houston, Los Angeles, and New York were primarily affected by the outbreak. Physicians reported 55,000 cases of people infected with rubeola. The age range of cases was from 5 months to 71 years. The severity of the epidemic was compounded by 123 deaths from measles. Another epidemic was reported in 2001 when 116 cases were reported to the CDC. The latest epidemic started in 2008, with measles outbreaks in several states. More than 70 cases were reported by May 2008 in the *Morbidity and Mortality Weekly Report,* a report on disease epidemiology that is published weekly by the CDC. It is believed that 54 of the people in these cases were exposed to measles during travel to Israel, Switzerland, and other countries.[4]

Epidemiologists must consider two risk factors when studying measles outbreaks. The first factor takes into consideration the characteristics of a person exposed to the virus. Typical characteristics for measles transmission include age, gender, and socioeconomic status. Another factor is the geographic location where the virus was originally contracted. Rubeola most commonly occurs in children and young adults. Outbreaks most frequently involve people aged 5 to 19 years. The next age group that commonly contracts rubeola is infants, followed by people over 20 years of age. This distribution of the disease is due to the fact that children are more likely to pass the virus to each other because they are more likely to be in close contact with one another in school and during play. In addition, children are less likely to practice proper hand washing after play and after using the restroom.

Gender seems to play a very small role in the epidemic spread of rubeola. However, women are more likely to be caretakers of children and thus are more prone to contracting measles from children. Measles is much more common in lower socioeconomic areas, where people are more likely to have limited access to medical care. As a consequence, people in this population are major carriers of the disease to other people. Poorer families also show higher incidences of malnutrition and undernutrition. These two consequences of poverty make children more susceptible to the rubeola virus. Plus, this makes it more likely for the disease to spread rapidly through the community, as shown in studies carried out by the CDC.[5]

The geographic location of exposure to rubeola is very important to public health officials. Different parts of the world are affected by dissimilar types of rubeola viruses. Scientists now categorize rubeola into eight genetically distinct categories or groups that developed from an original virus called the Edmonston strain, which is the most common group in the United States. Although each group is endemic to a particular part of the world, all groups of measles have been isolated from patients in the United States.

Group 1 is common in China, Russia, and the United Kingdom. The Philippines and many of the Pacific Islands have Group 2. Group 3 is found mostly in Japan and Thailand. North America and Europe characteristically harbor Groups 4 and 5. These groups are found in Austria, Germany, Greece, Italy, Spain, Ukraine, and the United Kingdom. Canada and Brazil also have outbreaks of Groups 4 and 5 measles. Group 6 is common in the African countries Cameroon, Gabon, Gambia, Kenya, and Zambia. People in Kenya, Pakistan, and South Africa typically contract Group 7 measles. Group 8 probably affects the most people in the world and is found mainly in China and Vietnam.

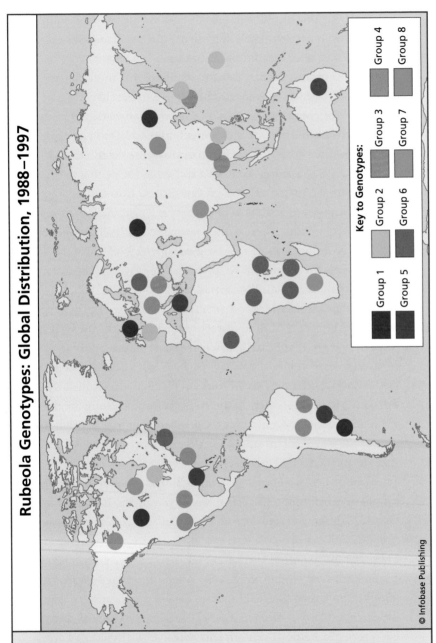

Rubeola Genotypes: Global Distribution, 1988–1997

Key to Genotypes:

Group 1 Group 2 Group 3 Group 4
Group 5 Group 6 Group 7 Group 8

© Infobase Publishing

Figure 5.2 This map shows the global distribution of the various rubeola genotypes.

Epidemiologists monitor outbreaks of different rubeola groups to get a better understanding of how the virus is distributed globally. Measles and other contagious diseases are easily transferred from one continent to another with international travel. The viral group is identified with each outbreak to determine the source of the rubeola. Appropriate preventative measures can then be taken to control the spread of the measles.

Different methods are used to control an endemic outbreak in contrast to an imported outbreak. Imported outbreaks are usually handled by developing guidelines that restrict the range of a disease. The WHO is revising the international health regulations to increase disease surveillance and prevention. Data about the distribution of rubeola groups also teaches epidemiologists how human migration patterns can affect the spread of other endemic diseases. This in turn helps governments develop preventative measures that stop the spread of a particular disease when it is introduced from another area. Preventative measures can include hygiene education and vaccination programs.

EPIDEMIOLOGY OF RUBELLA

Rubella is classified by epidemiologists as an infectious disease with a moderate degree of contagious potential. It spreads less rapidly than influenza and rubeola. The disease is most infectious when the rash is developing, after its 12-to-23–day incubation period. People in the early stages of the infection unknowingly become carriers and can spread the disease before the rash appears. Rubella is a notifiable disease according to the CDC and the WHO.

Rubella is generally transmitted in the mucus and saliva that is released when an infected person coughs or sneezes. The virus remains active for a short time in these bodily fluids. Tests show that the virus completely degrades within six hours after leaving the body. This means that close contact with the coughs and sneezes of an infected person is needed for maximum infectiveness. The contaminated fluids usually have to make direct contact with the other person's lining of the mouth or nose.

Children can also spread the virus by touching during casual contact or play. Fresh mucus or saliva on fomites has been shown to spread the rubella virus. Fomites become infectious when children cough and sneeze on toys or when they handle toys with contaminated hands. However, this is the least common means of infection. Half the effectiveness of the virus is lost every two hours on fomites. This is because half of the viruses degrade every two hours. A large number of viral particles must be initially present in mucus and saliva for it to be transmitted by touch and fomites. The virus is very vulnerable to dry surfaces and is easily killed by cleaning agents. Public health agencies recommend hand washing and appropriate household hygiene such as disinfecting surfaces to reduce the spread of rubella. There is no research showing data on the percentage in the reduction of virus spread when these practices are followed.

Passage of the rubella virus through the placenta is the most serious mode of spreading the disease. Pregnant women can pass the virus to their fetuses through the placenta. This in turn can lead to congenital rubella. The greatest chance of developing congenital rubella occurs before the thirteenth week of pregnancy. Up to 85 percent of fetuses infected during this period of pregnancy are born with some type of birth defect such as nervous system damage. There is a much lower probability of disease after the sixteenth week of pregnancy. Women who have not taken rubella preventative measures such as vaccination are highly susceptible to contracting the disease and passing it on to the fetus. The WHO is vigilant about ensuring the reduction of congenital rubella in developing countries. They promote educational and medical programs for eliminating congenital rubella. These programs help people recognize the disease and encourage them to vaccinate their children.

Rubella is a worldwide disease that usually appears as outbreaks during the spring and summer in cooler climates of the Northern and Southern hemispheres. In general, outbreaks occur primarily due to unvaccinated people with mild forms of the disease unknowingly spreading rubella. The disease is endemic to children between 3 and 10 years of age. Research shows that 50 percent of children worldwide have been exposed to the rubella virus. Other studies indicate that 5 to 10 percent of women of childbearing age are susceptible to a rubella infection.

The worst rubella outbreak in the United States reached epidemic proportions between 1964 and 1965. Physicians estimated that there were approximately 12.5 million cases of rubella and 20,000 cases of congenital rubella. This congenital rubella epidemic resulted in 3,580 babies born blind, 11,600 babies born deaf, and 1,800 babies born mentally retarded. More than 2,000 cases of encephalitis in adults also resulted. The morbidity was high in this epidemic. More than 13,000 babies died from rubella during that period.[6] Rubella outbreaks producing over 100 cases in a short period have occurred in Brazil, Greece, Italy, Korea, and the Netherlands. The WHO estimates that 123 countries report 800,000 rubella cases per year.

From 1996 through 1998, 14 small rubella outbreaks not exceeding 21 people per incident were reported in the United States. Most of those cases occurred in adults and were spread through the workplace. After those outbreaks, the average number of rubella cases reported between 1998 and 2000 was 272. This rate of measles occurrences dropped to an average of 13 cases per year between 2001 and 2004.[7]

Unlike rubeola, the rubella virus does not vary from one location to another. The virus is genetically consistent because it has stable DNA that does not change much over time. There is one variation of rubella virus that makes it more likely to cause human joint diseases. The virus is attracted to the tissues that make up joints and can damage the joints during the infection. This results in mobility problems and leads to physical handicaps. This makes it difficult for epidemiologists trying to track the source of an outbreak. Rubella in Hispanic immigrants residing in the United States has been on the increase, likely as a result of poverty preventing access to proper medical care. The CDC is having difficulties determining if the virus was contracted in Mexico or the United States.

6

Diagnosis, Treatment, and Prevention

In 2008, the CDC investigated 64 cases of measles between January 1 and April 25. This was largest number of measles cases reported for that period of time since 2001. This outbreak occurred in Arizona, California, Hawaii, Illinois, Michigan, Pennsylvania, Virginia, Michigan, and Wisconsin. Ten people claimed to have been exposed to measles while traveling outside of the United States. Finland, China, and various parts of the Middle East were visited. The CDC discovered that 63 of the people who contracted measles during this outbreak were not vaccinated. This outbreak verifies that measles has the potential of becoming a widespread plague if preventative measures are not taken.[1]

THEORY OF DIAGNOSING DISEASE

Some of the first means of diagnosing human disease are still being practiced today. Early Arabic, Egyptian, Greek, and Roman physicians learned to diagnose human diseases by recording the signs and symptoms of the different illnesses they encountered. They categorized diseases into different types based on differences and similarities. Until the nineteenth century, rubeola and rubella were recorded as different manifestations of the same disease because of the great overlap in signs and symptoms. In 1814, German physician George de Maton developed a means of discriminating between the two measles based on the course of the disease signs and symptoms. He used the severity of infection and the speed at which the disease progressed as the major distinguishing factors. Modern medical testing methods now make it simple for physicians to distinguish between the two measles.

Physicians today make a **presumptive diagnosis** of diseases such as rubeola and rubella by doing a physical examination. During the physical examination, the physician collects visual indicators of disease signs. The physician also records information about symptoms reported by the patient. From this information, the physician then narrows the presumptive diagnosis to likely disease conditions. The physician then orders clinical tests that give further information about the disease. Clinical tests include a large variety of medical testing done on body samples, which helps determine the cause of a disease. Blood and urine are the two most commonly collected body fluids used for clinical testing. Occasionally samples of cells and mucus are collected from the mouth and throat. This is commonly done to isolate microorganisms when an infectious disease is suspected.

Diseases are generally diagnosed using standard diagnostic guidelines established by medical and governmental organizations. The Clinical Surveillance Program (CSP) is a program for diagnosing disease that was established by the United States National Institutes of Health. It bases a diagnosis on a growing database of accurately reported cases. The MSH system of diagnosis was developed by the Management Sciences for Health. MSH is a private, nonprofit international organization that works on public health issues. The MSH definition provides scientific explanation of the disease that facilitates consistent diagnosis.

Serological evaluations on blood are the ideal clinical tests used for confirming measles. The presence of measles **antibodies** in the blood indicates the presence of the disease in the body. Antibody tests are performed by mixing the patient's blood with a known virus sample. The antibodies will only bind to a particular type of virus.

A diagnosis is followed by a **prognosis** and treatment. The prognosis is a prediction of the course and outcome of the disease condition. A treatment is the medical strategy used for alleviating disease. Physicians use the prognosis to determine an appropriate treatment based on the extent or severity of the disease. Treatments for infectious diseases involve using medications that enhance the immune system or kill the microorganism in the body. Other treatments are given to reduce the signs and symptoms of the disease. Various medications are used to lower a fever, reduce inflammation, and alleviate pain.

DIAGNOSIS OF RUBEOLA

The presumptive diagnosis of an early rubeola infection includes signs and symptoms that overlap with other infectious diseases and allergies. Physicians typically look for inflammation of the mucus membranes lining the nose and throat (**coryza**), **conjunctivitis**, and a severe cough. This

Figure 6.1 This child is being given an antibody test for rubeola and rubella. The presence of antibodies in her sample will indicate if she has been successfully vaccinated or if she already has immunity to these diseases. (© Geoff Tompkinson/Photo Researchers, Inc.)

should be accompanied by a fever greater than 101°F, or 38.3°C. Physicians also look for patient responses that indicate irritability, malaise, and **photophobia**. Photophobia is a condition in which the eyes are more sensitive than normal to light. Rubeola is often confused with a common childhood viral infection called erythema infectiosum at this point of the disease.

Rubeola is best indicated when Koplik's spots appear in the mouth, usually three to four days after the initial signs and symptoms. The Koplik's spots should be visible as grayish white sand-like dots that have a slight reddish outer ring. Sometimes the spots bleed. Physicians also look for a rash that spreads from the face and forehead to the chest one to two days after the appearance of the Koplik's spots. Inflammation of the tonsils and the lymph nodes in the neck support the diagnosis of a rubeola infection.

The Clinical Surveillance Program, which maintains a database of reported diseases, defines rubeola as "a childhood viral disease manifested as acute febrile illness associated with cough, coryza, conjunctivitis, spots on the buccal mucosa, and rash starting on the head and neck and spreading to the rest of the body."[2] If this definition is met, the physician reports the case and collects blood for clinical testing to confirm the diagnosis. Finding the rubeola virus in the serological testing satisfies the Management Sciences for Health definition of the disease. This private, nonprofit international public health organization further defines rubeola as "a highly contagious infectious disease caused by Morbillivirus, common among children but also seen in the non-immune of any age, in which the virus enters the respiratory tract via droplet nuclei and multiplies in the epithelial cells, spreading throughout the lymphatic system."[3] The blood test also helps identify the group of rubeola virus causing that infection.

The serological test results must also meet certain criteria to confirm rubeola. Two antibody tests are conducted to detect rubeola antibodies. One test is called the **complement-fixation test**. It looks for the ability of a person's antibodies to stimulate an immune response against the rubeola virus. The **hemagglutination-inhibition test** uses a different reaction to confirm the presence of rubeola antibodies. Both tests look for the presence of antibodies called **IgG** and **IgM** that specifically attach to the rubeola virus. These antibodies are produced by the body in response to a rubeola infection. However, a positive test for these antibodies can also indicate a person who had measles in the past and is currently not infected. Rubeola is confirmed when a large positive test is accompanied by early signs and symptoms of the disease.

Once rubeola is confirmed, physicians must be ready to make a prognosis, or prediction of the course and outcome of the disease, before giving a treatment. Rubeola can lead to dehydration and inflammation of the lung lining. It is also very likely for bacteria to invade the throat and lungs. Ear infections by bacteria and other viruses are also possible during measles. Severe outcomes of measles include damage to the heart, kidneys, and liver. Encephalitis occurs in 1 out of 1,000 cases in the usual population. People with weakened immune systems are more likely to suffer severe effects of a rubeola infection.

DIAGNOSIS OF RUBELLA

The CSP definition of rubella is less clear than its description of rubeola. It describes rubella as "an acute infectious disease caused by the rubella virus and most often affecting children and non-immune young adults, in which the virus enters the respiratory tract via droplet nuclei and spreads to the lymphatic system; usually benign; however transplacental infection of the fetus in the first trimester can cause death or severe developmental abnormalities leading to congenital rubella syndrome."[4] Similarly, the MSH defines rubella as "an acute, usually benign, infectious disease caused by the rubella virus and most often affecting children and non-immune young adults, in which the virus enters the respiratory tract via droplet nuclei and spreads to the lymphatic system."[5]

The CSP and MSH descriptions do not fully explain how to recognize rubella during the initial medical examination because the descriptions of the early signs and symptoms are too general. Patients with rubella at first seem to be suffering from a respiratory infection that appears at the early stages of the disease. The physician must check for a mild fever and swollen lymph nodes and tonsils. A rubella fever is typically no higher than 102°F, or 38.9°C. Very few people show a significant fever. The only noteworthy sign of rubella is the rash that forms. A rubella rash is composed of distinct red spots on the face that spread to the neck, chest, and extremities. These spots sometimes join together on the chest. As is the case with rubeola, the signs of rubella are also indicative of erythema. Unique to rubella are rashes that sometimes form on the roof of the mouth. This is one of the few sure signs of the disease.

Physicians must rely on serological testing to confirm rubella. Testing is most effective when the rash is evident because the formation of the rash corresponds with the appearance of rubella-specific antibodies. A complement-fixation test and hemagglutination-inhibition test are used to confirm the presence of rubella IgG and IgM antibodies. In mild cases, the test results must be evaluated to distinguish a past rubella infection from a current one. Usually a higher amount of antibodies in the blood indicates an active infection.

There is no diagnostic test for congenital rubella. It is assumed that the disease may occur if a woman tests positive for rubella antibodies during the first three months of pregnancy. A positive result on the serological test does not necessarily indicate an active rubella infection. The test is repeated throughout the pregnancy to see if the antibody levels rise. This gives an indication that an active infection in the mother may have been passed to the fetus. Suspected congenital rubella children are given a physical examination and serological test immediately after birth.

The prognosis for rubella in children and young adults varies greatly. In most cases, prognosis is good and patients progress to complete recovery. In moderate cases, the patient can develop fever and joint aches. This joint damage is due to an uncommon variety of rubella virus. The joint damage is short term and the pain subsides. Severe cases in rubella are atypical. In rare cases, physicians have reported swelling of glands in the cheeks or neck and 1 in 6,000 rubella patients develops inflammation of the brain that leads to permanent damage. Unfortunately, the prognosis for congenital rubella is usually very serious. Physicians must be prepared for babies being stillborn or born with birth defects.

TREATMENT OF THE MEASLES DISEASES

Currently there are very few effective cures for viral diseases. Most viral medications are intended to reduce the virus's ability to replicate; unfortunately, this type of treatment often alters or damages the body cells. Some physicians prescribe antibiotics for rubeola and rubella. The antibiotics have no effect on the virus, but they help prevent secondary bacterial infections, such as pneumonia, that can take hold while the immune system is weakened by rubella or rubeola.

Patients with rubeola and rubella are instructed to stay away from public places to prevent further spread of the disease. They are asked to stay home until all of their signs and symptoms have cleared up. Hospitalization is usually not required. Infected people are also told to get plenty of rest in a well-ventilated room with dim lighting. They must also take in sufficient amounts of fluids to prevent dehydration. Acetaminophen is given to control fever and reduce inflammation of the mucus membranes. Aspirin is not administered for treating viral diseases in children younger than 16 years of age. Aspirin can cause Reye's syndrome in children with viral infections.

Reye's syndrome is a potentially fatal disease that damages many body organs, particularly the brain and liver.

Rubeola and rubella patients are often told to take vitamin supplements to build up the immune system. They can also eat foods high in vitamins C and E, zinc, and chemicals called **flavonoids,** which are found naturally in plants and have been shown to slow the growth of viruses. They are commonly found in citrus fruits such as lemons and oranges.

Many people also use home remedies to facilitate recovery from rubeola and rubella. Herbal preparations that contain calendula flower, Echinacea, elderberry, ginseng, garlic, goldenseal, and spicebush are common remedies. However, physicians are not permitted to recommend these treatments. After preliminary research trials, the United States Food and Drug Administration found no compelling evidence that these treatments are effective or safe.

MEASLES PREVENTION

Prevention is the best means of keeping people safe from rubeola and rubella. **Immunization** was the first strategy used to contain both types of measles. Immunization is a strategy for improving the immune system's ability to fight an infection. **Immunoglobin** injections were the first immunization method used for rubeola and rubella. They were used over 100 years ago in the United States to treat a variety of diseases. Immunoglobins have been commonly given to ward off rubeola and rubella since the 1960s. **Immunoglobulins** are general antibodies that partially limit the spread of the virus. This treatment does not impart long-term protection against another infection.

Vaccinations are now known to be most effective against rubeola and rubella. A vaccine is a drug that induces a person's immune system to develop protection from a particular disease. Vaccines are usually made from components of the dead or weakened disease organism. They can be injected or taken orally. Most vaccines impart long-term protection against the disease. They cause the body to rapidly fight an infection before the organism spreads throughout the body. At first rubeola and rubella were prevented separately with two different types of vaccines, but now they are usually given together, along with a vaccine against mumps.

The first rubeola vaccine was developed by Charles Usher in 1960 and licensed for use in 1963. An improved rubeola vaccine was developed in 1968. The rubeola vaccine is generally called the measles vaccine, and it dramatically reduced the incidence of rubeola in the United States. This vaccine was eventually promoted worldwide to prevent rubeola epidemics. Immunization against rubeola is recommended for children 12 to 15 months of age. A second round of vaccination called a booster shot is recommended when a child is four to six years of age. This is necessary because a child's immune system is not fully developed and does not respond to the long-term effects of vaccination. The vaccine may not be effective in children under 12 months. Immunoglobin injections of **gamma globulin** are still used to prevent rubeola.

An effective rubella vaccine was approved for use in 1969. Immunization with the rubella vaccine is recommended for children aged 12 to 15 months, with a booster given when the child is four to six years of age. Vaccination is recommended also for pregnant women who have no immunity to the rubella virus. The frequency and size of rubella outbreaks declined significantly after the rubella vaccine became commonly administered. Data from the CDC indicates that rubella infections were reduced from 28 to 0.5 people per 100,000 population since the vaccine was introduced in 1963.[6]

In 1972, the rubella vaccine was combined with the measles and mumps vaccines to produce the measles/mumps/rubella (MMR) vaccine. Mumps is a viral infection of the salivary glands. This vaccine is injected below the skin in the fatty layer of tissue. MMR vaccine is administered for the same age groups

THE RUBELLA UMBRELLA

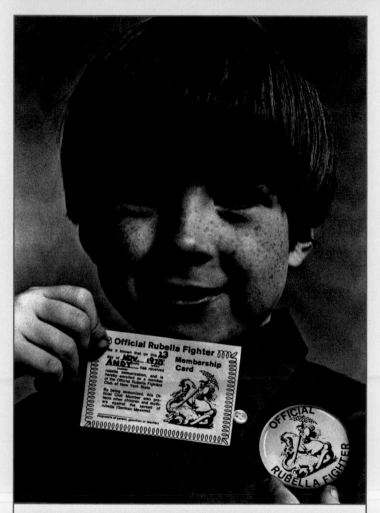

Figure 6.2   In the 1960s and 1970s, children who had been immunized against rubella were made official members of the Rubella Umbrella campaign. This was a program to make sure children received the vaccination; the program was promoted with buttons and membership cards. (Courtesy CDC)

Rubella became the topic of a public education campaign in the United States after a large outbreak in 1969. Public health offices recorded one of the largest number of annual rubella cases since the release of rubella vaccine in 1969. Physicians reported 57,686 cases of rubella to the CDC during the outbreak. This spurred the American government to develop a campaign encouraging people to seek rubella vaccination to protect children and pregnant women from the disease. It was known that the disease is less likely to reach epidemic proportions if most of the population is vaccinated. This promotion became known as the Rubella Umbrella campaign. Radio, magazine, and television advertisements encouraged parents to get their children vaccinated. Ads promoted the vaccination of pregnant women by stating the risks of birth defects. The phrase "Umbrella of Protection" has now become an established expression for disease prevention programs launched by the WHO. Significant reductions in vaccine-preventable diseases have been achieved over the past 15 years with global "umbrella" efforts.

as the separate measles and rubella vaccines. However, it is not recommended for adults who were previously vaccinated because it does not provide any more protection. Pregnant women are not given MMR vaccine until after they have given birth. Women must avoid getting pregnant for four weeks after getting MMR vaccine to avoid any possible complications to the pregnancy caused by vaccines.

The MMR vaccine does pose risks. A slight fever and a mild rash are the most common problems associated with the MMR vaccine. Some people develop joint pain and a reduced ability to heal. Severe reactions to the MMR vaccine can produce allergic reactions, brain damage, deafness, and seizures. These

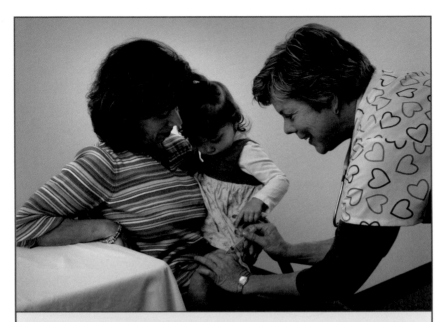

Figure 6.3 This child is receiving an intramuscular vaccination. The MMR vaccine is given to children using this method. (Courtesy CDC/ James Gathany)

reactions to the vaccine are very rare and are due to an overreaction of the immune system to the proteins in the vaccine.

A widespread misconception about the MMR vaccine developed in the United States in the 1990s, which later spread to other parts of the world. Many people believed that the vaccine caused **autism** and **Crohn's disease**. Autism is a brain disorder that affects a person's ability to communicate and relate to others. Crohn's disease is an inflammatory disease of the digestive system. The origin of this misconception is unknown.

In 2000, several governmental and scientific agencies in the United States reviewed all of the evidence about the dangers of MMR vaccine. The study ruled out any connection between MMR vaccine to autism or Crohn's disease. Other studies carried out globally by public health officials and physicians confirmed the American conclusions. Physicians continue to monitor the safety of MMR and other vaccines to ensure no links to long-term problems. Still, this misconception lingers and has caused many parents to avoid having their children vaccinated. It is believed that the incidence of rubeola and rubella increased globally as a result of the scare. Vaccination is the most reliable method of controlling rubeola and rubella. Both diseases can become annually epidemic in almost all nations if vaccination is discontinued.

7

Future Directions in Controlling Viral Diseases

Extensive measles vaccination programs carried out in the United States have dramatically reduced the incidence of measles cases. Measles has become so uncommon that medical students are unlikely to see a case during their education in medical school. In the United States alone, the incidence of measles has decreased fifty-fold since the introduction of vaccination.

Vaccination has not completely eradicated the disease, however. In 1999, scientists working for the Inspectorate of Health in the Netherlands discovered that vaccination programs merely redistribute the spread of measles. They discovered that measles outbreaks in urban areas occurred twice a year in the absence of vaccination. Vaccination programs produce small outbreaks that occur irregularly throughout the year. They believe this epidemiological change is due to small numbers of individuals who are unvaccinated. The unvaccinated people spread the disease to other unvaccinated populations slowly throughout the year. Vaccinated people are unaffected.

TRADITIONAL WAYS OF DEALING WITH VIRUSES
Viral diseases are the bane of physicians and public health officials. Ironically, the simplicity of viruses makes them very difficult to destroy. Unlike other microorganisms, viruses have no cellular structure that can be damaged with common disinfectants such as ammonia and antibacterial

soaps. Plus, they lack the metabolic machinery that can be disabled with antimicrobial chemicals. The small size of viruses makes them easily transmissible. They can pass through microscopic openings in surfaces and travel very long distances in the air. Certain viruses can remain infectious for years without any resources to keep them alive. Other viruses can stay dormant in dead cells and body samples almost indefinitely. In October 2005, scientists found a viable virus dating from the 1918 Spanish influenza pandemic in the body of a person who had been buried near Nome, Alaska.

Viral diseases are most successfully controlled with **prophylactic** methods. Prophylaxis means to avoid or prevent. Viral diseases are best thwarted by keeping the virus from contacting the cells of susceptible people. Strategies for preventing viruses from entering the body vary greatly. Cleanliness and personal hygiene are the simplest ways of keeping viruses from invading the body. Proper cleanliness removes viral particles attached to dust and to the surfaces of objects. Personal hygiene includes hand washing and covering the mouth when coughing or sneezing. Hand-washing disinfectants must be able to deactivate viruses or rid them from the skin. This must be accomplished without damaging the body. Many antiviral skin disinfectants used for home and school are a mixture of various alcohols and soaps. They help remove the viruses from the skin and dehydrate any existing viruses. These mixtures are mostly effective against enveloped viruses. Hospitals and food establishments use stronger skin disinfectants that contain mildly toxic metals, **organic compounds**, and salts. They interfere with the function of the viral capsid and genetic material.

Coughing and sneezing into tissues is a good way of reducing the spread of airborne viruses. This prevents the spread of viruses in two ways. First, it traps viruses that were carried out of the body in the mucus and the saliva. Airborne viruses such as rubeola and rubella spread readily through coughing and sneezing. Coughing and sneezing into tissues also keeps mucus

Figure 7.1   Handwashing is a simple, yet important, technique to stop the spread of many diseases, including rubella and rubeola. (© Mariusz Szachowski/Shutterstock images)

and saliva off of the hands. Rubeola and rubella are commonly transmitted through contact with contaminated hands. However, the tissues must be disposed of properly to keep the fluids from coming in contact with other people. If tissues are not available, coughing or sneezing into the elbow instead of the hands is recommended.

Strong disinfectants can be used to reduce the number of viruses on surfaces. Common **antiviral** surface disinfectants include bleach and phenol, which disable the virus by decomposing the capsid, envelope, and genetic material. Unfortunately, these chemicals are irritating to the skin and mucous membranes. Thus, they must be used carefully to prevent harm.

Medical supply industries and hospitals must sometimes use other prophylactic techniques to control the spread of viruses. Clothing and instruments that may have come in contact with viruses are sterilized using various methods. Autoclaves are vessels that use high-pressure steam to sterilize many types of medical instruments. They can reach temperatures of 250°F, or 121°C. Capsid proteins and genetic material are disrupted at this temperature. Vessels related to autoclaves sterilize clothing and delicate instruments using toxic gases such as ethylene oxide, which makes the viral chemistry inoperative.

The removal of dust and other particles in the air is another way to ensure cleanliness. Almost all hospitals use special heating and air conditioning systems that remove dust or sterilize the air. Air circulating through clinics and hospitals passes through special high-efficiency particulate air (HEPA) filters that trap and collect small particles. When used properly, they can remove more than 99 percent of the dust and microorganism particles circulating in the air. Many air conditioning systems have built-in ultraviolet (UV) systems that degrade the genetic material of viruses that pass through

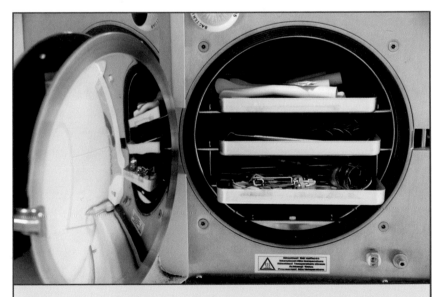

Figure 7.2 An autoclave is a sterilizing machine that cleans instruments using pressurized steam. Autoclaves are used in medical and dental offices, as well as in research facillities. (© Tomasz Kozakiewiez/Phototake)

the system. UV systems can be integrated with HEPA traps to kill and remove viruses.

Vacuum cleaners are also equipped with HEPA filters. This prevents dust on the floor from entering air during vacuuming. HEPA filters that specifically remove viruses have been developed. HEPA breathing masks can also be used to prevent the passage of viruses from one person to another. The masks can be worn by medical workers or by infected patients. These masks are much more sophisticated than surgical masks and the dust masks that are sold at hardware stores.

Vaccination is considered a backup prophylactic that works after the virus has made contact with the body. It prevents the virus from successfully replicating in the body. **Passive vaccines** enhance the immune system for the duration of a disease. They are composed of immunoglobins that help remove viruses from the body. Immunoglobins direct the body to attack the virus. Passive vaccination is primarily used to ward off a variety of microorganisms and is useful during a rapid disease outbreak. **Active vaccines** provide long-term protection from viruses. They are composed of components of the microorganism. Active vaccination stimulates the immune system to fight off a specific infectious disease. Most active vaccines provide protection for several years. Vaccines are usually administered as injections into the blood or underneath the skin surface. Some are delivered as a pill. Rubeola and rubella vaccines are delivered as an injection into the muscle.

Antiviral medications are used to control certain viral diseases if the person is already infected. Currently there are about 50 commonly used antiviral agents, some of which may be useful for treating rubeola and rubella. These are all approved by the federal government and are only available by prescription from a physician. Traditional antiviral drugs interfere with the replication of viruses once an infection has progressed. Antiviral drugs have many modes of action. Certain antiviral agents keep viruses from attaching to cells. The virus cannot replicate unless it enters a cell. This gives the immune system adequate time to readily remove the viruses from the body fluids. Other antiviral drugs prevent the uncoating of the viral capsid. This prevents the genetic material from being replicated in the cell.

Other types of antiviral medications alter the cell's metabolism in a way that affects the virus. Certain drugs use this mechanism to prevent the viral genetic material from replicating. Another group of medications interfere with capsid or envelope formation. This prevents the viruses from maturing. They can also work by causing incomplete viruses to exit the cell. The incomplete viruses are incapable of infecting other cells. Unfortunately, most antiviral drugs can harm the body. They can damage blood cells, the kidneys, and the liver. Certain antiviral drugs interfere with **nerve cell** function.

Other therapies are often given to supplement antiviral drugs. Immune system chemicals such as interleukins are given to boost the immune system's ability to remove viruses. An interleukin called interferon is regularly used to treat viral hepatitis. Alternative antiviral treatments are sometimes recommended to enhance traditional treatments. Many types of plants contain chemicals that have mild antiviral activities. They are most effective in enhancing the body's ability to ward off a viral invasion. Most alternative treatments boost the immune system. They help the body remove viruses that have not yet entered cells or have recently exited an infected cell. Other alternative treatments interfere with a virus's ability to adhere to cells. This restricts the replication rate of the viruses. In addition, they help the mucous membranes remove viruses before the viruses have a chance to enter the cells. These therapies might prove effective against rubeola and rubella.

FUTURE VIRAL TREATMENT

Scientists are constantly investigating new prophylactic techniques for controlling the spread of viruses. Some of the discoveries make their way into everyday products. New strategies are now applied for controlling airborne viruses such as rubeola and rubella. Kleenex was the first company to market prophylactic tissues for household use. Disinfectant chemicals layered in the center of the tissue trap and decompose the envelopes of certain viruses. They are most effective against the highly contagious cold and influenza viruses. The company claims that 99 percent of the viruses are deactivated within 15 minutes, making it simple to dispose of the tissue without spreading infection. Unfortunately, these tissues are not officially recognized by the FDA as an efficient method of controlling rubeola and rubella.

Other antiviral materials have been developed by embedding antiviral chemicals into fabrics, plastic, and rubber. In 2001, researchers at Baxter International Incorporated patented a way of permanently binding antiviral chemicals called phenols to different types of materials. The antiviral chemicals degrade viruses that come in contact with the material. Very little of the chemicals can leak out, making the materials safe and useful for a long period of time. There are plans to use these antiviral materials to produce disposable medical instruments, hospital bedding, and medical clothing. These products will be most effective on enveloped viruses such as rubeola and rubella.

A patent for an antiviral drug called ribavirin, which is effective against measles was awarded in 2000. The drug contains small proteins that inhibit rubeola replication. It works by preventing the virus from entering cells. This leaves the virus susceptible to rapid removal by the immune system. As of 2008, the drug is still undergoing clinical tests for effectiveness and safety, and it may take several years before it is released for use by physicians.

Several researchers developed antiviral nasal drops and sprays against cold and influenza viruses. The products contain cell surface proteins that viruses use to enter a cell and work by blocking the virus's ability to adhere to cells in the nose and throat. The surface proteins in the products attach to the viruses, keeping the viruses in the mucus and saliva. A similar strategy might be used to keep rubeola and rubella from entering body cells. Another type of nasal and throat spray uses antibodies to prevent airborne viral infections. Various types of immunoglobins were shown effective at reducing infections with cold and influenza viruses. Future developments need to be made for a similar product to control rubeola and rubella.

A new biotechnology method may one day become a viable substitute for traditional antiviral drugs. **Interference RNA** uses a specially designed RNA molecule to disrupt or modify a cellular process without harming healthy cells. In 2000, Canadian researchers produced an interference RNA that blocked rubella replication. German researchers in 2006 developed an interference RNA that prevented synthesis of the rubeola genome. Genetically modified cells have also been turned into **viricides**. These cells are designed to seek out and destroy virus-infected cells. They kill the cells before the virus can spread throughout the body. Currently they work best on the AIDS virus, but may one day prove effective on rubella or rubeola viruses.

The new science of **nanotechnology** may be the answer to the next generation of viral prophylaxis. Nanotechnology is a branch of science and engineering that develops extremely small devices. Researchers are proposing using nanotechnology to build novel microscopic virus-killing machines. These new developments are being called nanoviricides. One future nanoviricide will act like a guided missile inserted in the body that binds to viral surface proteins. It is hoped that this nanoviricide missile will elicit an immune response before the virus causes a serious infection. They will play the same role as passive immunization. However, these missiles can be targeted at particular types of viruses.

Another type of nanoviricide acts like a drug delivery system. It borders on being prophylactic and antiviral. Scientists have already created artificial cell-like spheres called

micelles. Micelles can be filled with different types of chemicals, including any type of medicine for curing a variety of diseases. Special proteins can be placed on the surface of a micelle so it leaks out the chemicals at a controlled time. Modified micelles are currently being turned into artificial replacement glands that deliver hormones into the blood. Antiviral micelles are being designed to attach to cells infected with a particular type of virus. The micelle inserts antiviral drugs only into the infected cell. This will reduce the toxic effects of traditional antiviral drugs.

New ways of delivering vaccines are also being developed. The science of **biotechnology** is opening the door for a strategy called edible vaccination. Researchers have successfully introduced genes for making vaccines into plants. The earliest antiviral edible vaccines were developed for agricultural animals. One patented edible vaccine for use in pigs protects against a hepatitis virus and a **gastroenteritis** virus. The vaccine is produced in fruit, vegetable, and grain products that go into pig feed. Edible vaccines for cattle are already in use in many countries. They are produced in grains and potatoes. Bananas and potatoes are being investigated as sources of edible vaccines for humans. It is hoped to combat a variety of contagious human viruses using edible vaccines. Investigations show that they could be effective against rubeola and rubella.

The early diagnosis of viral diseases has also benefited from biotechnology. A process called **polymerase chain reaction** (PCR) is being refined to diagnose viral diseases. PCR is a procedure for making multiple copies of genetic material from very small samples. It was developed to assist with the identification of genetic material samples. Usually it takes a fairly large sample of genetic material to conduct a genetic analysis. PCR makes it possible to multiply minute amounts of genetic material into a larger sample. Viral diseases are usually diagnosed by detecting specific antibodies in the body fluids. However,

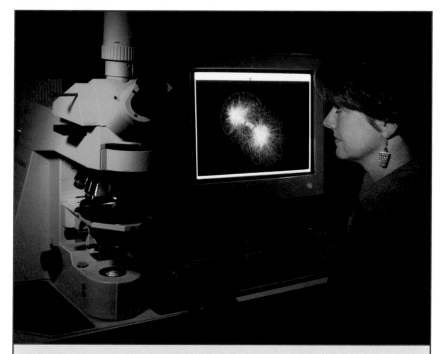

Figure 7.3   Dr. Julie Ahringer, shown here, is studying interference RNA using a microscope. Interference RNA is being studied for its use in fighting viral diseases, such as rubella and rubeola. (© Brian Bell/Photo Researchers, Inc.)

the antibodies are produced well after the infection has started and may even have spread to other people. PCR techniques are being developed to collect and amplify the genetic material of viruses, including the measles viruses. Infections can be caught prior to causing harm and before the disease is transmitted.

An emerging medical philosophy called **systems biology** is taking a new approach to treating viral diseases. Systems biology investigates how an organism's genetic material interacts with the environment and under disease conditions. Many factors, including lifestyle and diet, are taken into account when developing systems biology approaches. Studies are currently being conducted to better understand how human cells respond to a viral invasion. This knowledge is translated into specific treatments that can cure the viral disease before it harms the body. It can also lead to better prophylactic therapies that stop the virus from replicating without harming the cell. Any advances in the diagnosis, prevention, and treatment of viral diseases will prove useful for controlling rubeola and rubella. One day it may even be possible to eradicate the measles diseases.

Chapter 3

1. R.W. Sutter, L.E. Markowitz, J.M. Bennetch, W. Morris, E.R. Zell, and S.R. Preblud, "Measles among the Amish: a comparative study of measles severity in primary and secondary cases in households," *Journal of Infectious Diseases* 163, 1 (January 1991): 12–6.

2. V. DeJohn Anderson, *Creatures of Empire: How Domestic Animals Transformed Early America*, (New York: Oxford University Press, 2006).

Chapter 4

1. J. Vögele, "Information, Urbanization and the urban mortality change in Imperial Germany," *Health & Place*, 6,1 (2000): 41–55.

2. About.com, "Deafness Blog—Deafness from German Measles Hereditary?" (Tuesday October 2, 2007), http://deafness.about.com/b/2007/10/02/deafness-from-german-measles-hereditary.htm.

Chapter 5

1. Health Protection Surveillance Centre. "NDSC Warns of Measles Epidemic Because Irish Children are Not Being Vaccinated," (July 13, 2000), http://www.ndsc.ie/hpsc/PressReleases/2000PressReleases/MainBody,539,en.html.

2. R.M. Anderson and R.M. May, *Infectious Diseases of Humans*, (Oxford, UK: Oxford University Press, 1991), 10.

3. G.C. Kohn (ed.), *Encyclopedia of Plague and Pestilence*, (New York: Facts On File, 1995).

4. Advisory Committee on Immunization Practices, "Summary Report 2008," Department of Health and Human Services Centers for Diseases Control and Prevention.

5. Centers for Disease Control and Prevention, *Morbidity and Mortality Weekly Report* 52, 11(March 21, 2003): 228–229.

6. J.J. Witte, A.W. Karchmer, G. Case, et al., "Epidemiology of rubella." *American Journal Of Diseases Of Children*, 118 (1969): :107–111.

7. Centers for Disease Control and Prevention, "Achievements in Public Health: Elimination of Rubella and Congenital Rubella Syndrome—United States, 1969–2004," *Morbidity and Mortality Weekly Report*, 54, 11 (March 25, 2005): 279–282.

Chapter 6

1. Centers for Disease Control and Prevention, "Measles—United States, January 1–April 25, 2008," *Morbidity and Mortality Weekly Report*, 57, 18 (May 9, 2008): 494–498.

2. Family Practice Notebook, "Measles," http://www.fpnotebook.com/ID/Virus/Msls.htm.

3. W.A.N. Dorland, *Dorland's Pocket Medical Dictionary, 28th Edition* (Philadelphia: Saunders, 2008).

4. Family Practice Notebook, "Rubella,": http://www.fpnotebook.com/ID/Virus/Rbl.htm.

5. W.A.N. Dorland, *Dorland's Pocket Medical Dictionary, 28th Edition* (Philadelphia: Saunders, 2008).

6. Centers for Disease Control and Prevention, "Measles, Mumps, and Rubella—Vaccine Use and Strategies for Elimination of Measles, Rubella, and Congenital Rubella Syndrome and Control of Mumps: Recommendations of the Advisory Committee on Immunization Practices (ACIP)," *Morbidity and Mortality Weekly Report*, 47, RR-8 (May 22, 1998): 1–57.

Glossary

active vaccine—A treatment that stimulates the immune system to fight off a specific infectious disease.

adsorption—The process of sticking onto something.

agent—A chemical or organism that carries out a particular function.

allergy—A condition in which the immune system overreacts to a substance in the body.

antibody—An immune system chemical that attaches to foreign substances in the body.

antigen—Any substance that can produce an immune response.

antihistamine—A drug that reduces the inflammation response.

antimicrobial—Something that kills microorganisms.

antiviral—A disinfectant treatment that destroys viruses.

apoptosis—A situation in which cells can program their own death using a strategy called programmed cell death.

arbovirus—A large group of viruses spread by insects to animals and plants.

attachment proteins—Viral capsid proteins that help a virus complete its life cycle.

autism—A brain disorder that affects a person's ability to communicate and relate to others.

autoclave—A vessel that uses high-pressure steam to sterilize medical instruments.

bacteria—A primitive single-celled microorganism that feeds on dead matter or lives as a pathogen on animals and plants.

bacteriophage—A virus that infects bacteria.

biochemistry—The science of understanding the chemistry of cells and the body.

biogenesis—A principle based on the discovery that life comes from preexisting life.

biotechnology—The science of using naturally occurring or modified living organisms for specific medical or technological uses.

bird flu—Also known as avian influenza, it is a type of virus that harms the respiratory system of birds and can be spread to other animals.

bubonic plague—A bacterial disease spread by fleas, also called black plague.

capsomere—A subunit protein that makes up a viral capsid.

cardiovascular—Associated with the heart and blood vessels.

carrier—A person or animal that does not show a disease but that possesses the infectious agent.

case-control study—A retrospective epidemiology study done on a new disease.

casing—A covering that encloses an object or organism.

cataract—A clouding of the lens of the eye that makes vision very blurry.

cell division—The process of replicating cells or making gametes for sexual reproduction.

cell membrane—A lipid and protein covering that encloses the cytoplasm of a cell.

cerebral palsy—A brain condition that affects muscle control.

chemotherapy—A treatment of disease using poisonous chemicals that kill cells.

complement-fixation test—A clinical test used to look for antibodies against a particular infectious disease.

congenital rubella syndrome—A serious disease that results when a fetus is infected with the rubella virus.

conjunctiva—A thin skin-like layer covering the front surface of the eye.

conjunctivitis—Inflammation of the conjunctiva.

contagious—A disease that is easily spread.

corrosive—A chemical that breaks apart or wears away materials gradually by chemical action.

coryza—Inflammation of the mucus membranes lining the nose and throat.

Crohn's disease—An inflammatory disease of the digestive system.

crystal—A tightly packed chemical structure with regularly arranged atoms.

crystallography—The science of using x-rays to analyze the chemistry and shape of crystal structures.

Glossary

cytoplasm—Cellular material that is within the cell membrane.

deoxyribonucleic acid—The chemical that makes up the genetic material of cells.

diffuse—Spread throughout the body.

distemper—A deadly viral disease of many animals that damages all of the body organs.

DNA—An acronym for deoxyribonucleic acid. It makes up the genetic material.

DNA virus—A virus with DNA as its genetic material.

double-stranded—A term used to describe nucleic acid molecules that are made up of two chains of nucleic acids attached side-by-side.

eclipse phase—A stage of viral infection that follows uncoating, in which the virus hides in the cell.

electron microscope—A powerful microscope that uses electrons to magnify an object.

electron—A negatively charged particle that orbits the nucleus of an atom.

encephalitis—Any disease that causes damage and swelling of the brain.

endemic—The regular presence of a disease or infectious agent within a certain population of people.

envelope—A covering on the virus that resembles a cell membrane.

enveloped viruses—Viruses that possess an envelope that surrounds the capsid.

enzyme—A protein that carries out specific chemical reactions.

epidemic—The occurrence of more cases of disease than expected in a given area or among a specific group of people within a certain period of time.

epidemiology—The study of the occurrence and frequency of disease in populations.

epithelial cells—Flat cells that line major body systems.

etiologic population—The proportion of all disease cases that are associated with an exposure or risk.

exposure—A risk factor in the environment such as a thing or situation that brings the organism in contact with person.

filamentous—Describes a cell or virus shaped like a rope.

filtering—The process of removing solid particles from a liquid using a filter.

flavonoid—A chemical found in plants that slows the growth of viruses.

fomite—A nonliving vector.

fungus—A diverse group of organisms usually composed of cells formed into branched filaments. Fungi feed primarily on decaying matter. The plural of fungus is fungi.

gamete—A cell involved in sexual reproduction.

gamma globulin—A type of immunoglobin used for viral immunization.

gastroenteritis—A disease causes inflammation of the digestive system.

genes—Sequences of DNA that represent fundamental units of heredity.

genetic disorder—A condition caused partly or completely by a defect in one or more genes.

genetics—The study of DNA structure, function, and inheritance.

genome—The complete genetic material of an organism.

genus—A scientific category representing groups of similar organisms.

helix—A spiral structure that is shaped like a spring.

hemagglutinin—A protein that binds to red blood cells and causes them to clump.

hemagglutination-inhibition test—A clinical test used to look for antibodies against a particular infectious disease.

histamines—Immune system chemicals produced by blood cells.

hormone—A chemical signal that causes cells to carry out a particular function.

IgG—A type of antibody found in the serum during a disease.

IgM—A type of antibody found in the serum during a disease.

immune response—A set of reactions the body uses to attack and remove foreign substances that enter the body.

Glossary

immunization—A process by which protection to an infectious disease or cancer is administered.

immunoglobin—An antibody.

immunoglobulin—A protein used to battle foreign substances.

inclusion body—An empty nucleocapsid produced in cells infected with certain viruses.

incubation period—The time from contact with an infectious organism to the first signs or symptoms of disease.

interference RNA—A technique that uses RNA molecules to disrupt or modify cellular processes.

interferon—A type of interleukin used to combat viral infections.

interleukin—A chemical that protects the body from viral infections.

Koplik's spots—Small red spots with bluish centers that appear inside the mouth with rubeola.

latent period—The time between the measurable onset of disease and detection of the disease.

lymph nodes—Structures that help the body fight disease and assist with the repair of tissues.

lysis—The breakdown and subsequent death of a cell.

macular—Discoloration of the skin.

maculopapular—Refers to a discolored skin rash.

malaise—A general condition of not feeling well.

maturation phase—The stage of viral infection in which new viruses are assembled.

metabolism—A series of chemical reactions that carry out the functions of a cell and an organism.

micelle—An artificial cell-like structure.

microorganisms—An organism of microscopic or submicroscopic size, especially a bacterium or protozoan.

mitochondria—Structures within a cell responsible for the conversion of food into cell energy.

molecule—The name given to a chemical made up of two or more atoms.

morbidity—Any illness resulting from a disease.

Morbillivirus—A genus of viruses that contains the measles virus.

mortality—A measure of the occurrence of death from a disease in a particular population of people during a particular period of time.

mucus—The substance that is secreted as a protective lubricant coating by cells and glands of the mucous membranes.

mutation—A genetic change that occurs in an organism.

nanotechnology—A branch of science and engineering that develops extremely small devices.

negative-sense RNA—A type of RNA that requires special conditions to replicate.

nerve cell—A cell that receives and sends messages from the body to the brain and back to the body.

nucleic acid—A complex molecule associated with the structure and function of genetic material. DNA and RNA are composed of nucleic acids.

nucleocapsid—An inner capsid that directly surrounds the viral genome.

nucleotide—A nucleic acid attached in a chain to other nucleic acids.

nucleus—A structure in eukaryotic cells that contains the genetic material.

organic compounds—Chemicals derived from living organisms.

otitis media—An infection of the middle part of the ear.

pandemic—A widespread disease.

paramyxoviridae—A large category of viruses that contains the *Morbillivirus* genus.

parasite—An organism that lives in or on the living tissue of a host organism at the expense of that host.

particle—A name given to viruses and related organisms that do not possess the major properties of life.

passive vaccine—An immunoglobin treatment that enhances the immune system for the duration of a disease.

Glossary

photophobia—A condition in which the eyes are more sensitive than normal to light.

placenta—An organ that nourishes the developing fetus in the uterus.

polymerase chain reaction—A biotechnology procedure for making multiple copies of genetic material from very small samples.

positive-sense RNA—A type of RNA that contains genetic information in a conventional format.

presumptive diagnosis—The probable diagnosis of a disease, derived from a physical examination.

preventive medicine—A branch of medicine that includes practices that help people avoid disease and promote health.

prognosis—A prediction of the course and outcome of the disease condition.

prophylactic—Strategies used to prevent the spread of disease.

prospective epidemiology—A technique used to determine whether a disease may develop in a person or a population in the future.

protein—A complex molecule made up of amino acids; essential to cell structure and function.

protists—Microscopic organisms that have a nucleus and are generally composed of a single cell.

pyrogen—A substance that causes the elevation of body temperature.

receptor—A protein that binds to specific types of chemicals.

red blood cells—Cells in the blood that carry oxygen.

release phase—The final stage of viral infection in which new viruses are released from the cell.

retina—A part of the eye that contains the visual cells.

retrospective epidemiology—Investigation of a disease after it already happened.

risk factor—A term explaining the circumstances that cause a person to develop a disease.

RNA—Ribonucleic acid, which is a chemical similar to DNA, is a nucleic acid involved in the production of proteins.

RNA virus—A virus with RNA as its genetic material.

Rubivirus—The genus of the rubella virus.

scurvy—A night blindness disease caused by a lack of vitamin C or ascorbic acid.

self-assembling—The ability of a chemical to form complex structures on their own accord by attaching to one another or to other chemicals.

serological—Refers to clinical tests carried out on blood.

sexual reproduction—A process that involves fusing two gametes to produce a new organism with blended characteristics of the parents.

sign—Any evidence of the presence of a disease that can be measured or detected.

single-stranded—A term used to describe nucleic acid molecules made up of only one chain.

subacute sclerosing panencephalitis—Progressive damage to the brain usually caused by viral infections.

symptom—Evidence of a disease as perceived by the patient.

syncytium—A condition caused by cells fusing together.

syndrome—A disease condition that affects many body organs.

synthesis—The process of building new molecules.

systems biology—A branch of medicine that investigates how an organism's genetic material interacts with the environment and under diseased conditions.

teratogenic—The ability to cause birth defects.

teratogen—Something that causes birth defects.

Togaviridae—A group of viruses that contains the *Rubivirus* and *Alphavirus*.

tumors— Abnormal growths of tissue resulting from uncontrolled, progressive multiplication of cells and serving no physiological function.

ultraviolet light—A high-energy light that can damage many types of molecules.

umbilical cord—A cord that connects the fetus at the navel to the placenta.

uncoating—A stage of viral infection in which the capsid is removed from the virus.

Glossary

urogenital system—Body structure involved in the removal of body wastes from the blood and in reproduction.

vaccination—The process by which a person's immune system is induced to develop protection from a particular disease.

vector-assisted transmission—Spread of a disease by a vector.

viricide—A substance that disables viruses.

virology—The study of viruses and viral diseases.

virulent—Something that is extremely infectious or poisonous.

white blood cells—A group of blood cells involved in the immune response.

Books

Abbas, Abul K., and Andrew H. Lichtman. *Basic Immunology: Functions and Disorders of the Immune System.* New York: Saunders, 2008.

Alberts, Bruce, Julian Lewis, Martin Raff, Alexander Johnson, and Keith Roberts. *Molecular Biology of the Cell.* London, England: Taylor & Francis, Inc., 2002.

Alcamo, I. Edward. *DNA Technology: The Awesome Skill.* Philadelphia: Elsevier Science & Technology Books, 2000.

Banatvala, Jangu, and Catherine Peckham. *Rubella Viruses,* Volume 15 (Perspectives in Medical Virology). Amsterdam, Netherlands: Elsevier Science, 2007.

Bauman, Robert. *Microbiology.* San Francisco: Pearson Education, 2002.

Brooks, George F. *Medical Microbiology,* 24th ed. (Jawetz, Melnick, & Adelberg's Medical Microbiology). Dubuque, Iowa: McGraw-Hill, 2007.

Carter, John, and Venetia Saunders. *Virology: Principles and Applications.* Hoboken: Wiley, 2007.

Corlett, William Thomas. *A Treatise on the Acute, Infectious Exanthemata; Including Variola, Rubeola, Scarlatina, Rubella, Varicella and Vaccinia.* Whitefish, Mont.: Kessinger Publishing, 2007.

Diamond, Jared. *Guns, Germs and Steel: The Fates of Human Societies.* New York: Norton, W. W. & Company, Inc., 1999.

Goodsell, David S. *Bionanotechnology.* Hoboken: Wiley-Liss, 2004.

Ratner, Mark A., and Daniel Ratner. *Nanotechnology: A Gentle Introduction to the Next Big Idea.* Indianapolis: Prentice Hall PTR, 2002.

Shmaefsky, Brian R. *Applied Anatomy and Physiology: A Case Study Approach.* St Paul: EMC/Paradigm, 2007.

Shmaefsky, Brian R. *Biotechnology 101* (Science 101 series). Westport, Conn.: Greenwood Press, 2006.

Web Sites

Biotechnology Industries Organization
http://www.bio.org

Centers for Disease Control and Prevention
http://www.cdc.gov

Further Resources

Cold Spring Harbor Laboratory
http://www.cshl.org

HealthLink. Medical College of Wisconsin
http://healthlink.mcw.edu

Internet Public Library History of Medicine
http://www.ipl.org/div/subject/browse/hea30.00.00

Martin Memorial Health System
http://www.mmhs.com

Mayo Clinic
http://www.mayoclinic.com

MedIndia
http://www.medindia.net/healthnews/Measles-news.asp

Medline Plus. A service of the U.S. National Library of Medicine and the
National Institutes of Health
http://www.nlm.nih.gov

Microbiology Bytes
http://www.microbiologybytes.com/introduction/index.html

National Library of Medicine
http://www.nlm.nih.gov

Toronto Public Health, Measles Fact Sheet
http://www.toronto.ca/health/pdf/measles_factsheet.pdf

Toronto Public Health
http://www.toronto.ca/health/immune_mmr.htm

Virology Journal
http://www.virology.net

World Health Organization
http://www.who.int

Index

Index

immunoglobulins, 82
inclusion bodies, 42
incubation period, 44–45
Infectious Diseases of Humans: Dynamics and Control (Andersen and May), 61
influenza, 30, 32
Inspectorate of Health (the Netherlands), 88
interference RNA, 95
interferon, 93
interleukins, 45, 93
International Committee on Taxonomy, 40
international health regulation, 71
Ireland and rubeola, 61
Ivanovski, Dimitri, 9

kidney damage, 79
Kleenex tissues, 94
Koch, Robert, 62, 62
Koch's Postulates, 62
Koplik's spots, 45, 78
kuru, 10

latent period, 65
Lederberg, Joshua, 13
Lee, W. Robert, 50
leprosy, 30–31, 35
liver damage, 79

Luria, Salvador, 13
lymph nodes, 55
lysis, 23

maculopapular, 57
malaise, 56
malaria, 30, 32
malnutrition, 30
Management Sciences for Health (MSH), 76, 78, 79–80
Marschalck, Peter, 50
maturation phase, 22–23
May, Robert, 61
measles, 27, 35–37, 38. *See also* preventative measures; rubella; rubeola; treatment of diseases; vaccinations
measles/mumps/rubella (MMR) vaccine, 83, 85–87
medications, antiviral, 92–93
mental retardation, 60
metabolism, 14
mice as disease vectors, 31
micelles, 96
microorganisms, 27
mitochondria, 53
MMR vaccine. *See* measles/mumps/rubella vaccine

molecules, 14
morbidity, 65
Morbidity and Mortality Weekly Report, 68
Morbillivirus, 40
mortality, 65
MSH. *See* Management Sciences for Health
mucus, 45
mumps, 83
mutation, 39

nanotechnology, science of, 95
nanoviricides, 95
nasal drops/sprays, 94
National Disease Surveillance Centre (Ireland), 61
National Institutes of Health, 76
Native Americans and infectious diseases, 67, 68
negative-sense RNA, 19
nerve cell function, 93
the Netherlands and measles, 88
nose inflammation, 77–78
nucleic acids, 12–13
nucleocapsid, 18
nucleotide, 42
nucleus, 30

Index

Index

Brian Shmaefsky, Ph.D., is a professor of biology at Lone Star College—Kingwood near Houston, Texas. He completed his undergraduate studies in biology at Brooklyn College in New York and his masters and doctoral studies at Southern Illinois University at Edwardsville. Dr. Shmaefsky also completed graduate work in environmental physiology at the University of Illinois and Rocky Mountain Biological Laboratory. His research emphasis is currently in environmental toxicology issues and sustainable development. Dr. Shmaefsky has many publications on science teaching and several books on topics such as biotechnology, human anatomy and physiology, and infectious diseases. He is very active internationally in environmental policy groups and has ongoing projects in Mexico and the Philippines. Dr. Shmaefsky has two children, Timothy and Kathleen, and lives in Kingwood, Texas.

About the Consulting Editor

Hilary Babcock, M.D., M.P.H., is assistant professor of medicine at Washington University School of Medicine and the medical director of occupational health for Barnes-Jewish Hospital and St. Louis Children's Hospital. She received her undergraduate degree from Brown University and her M.D. from the University of Texas Southwestern Medical Center at Dallas. After completing her residency, chief residency, and infectious diseases fellowship at Barnes-Jewish Hospital, she joined the faculty of the infectious disease division. She completed an M.P.H. in public health from St. Louis University School of Public Health in 2006. She has lectured, taught, and written extensively about infectious diseases, their treatment, and their prevention. She is a member of numerous medical associations and is board certified in infectious diseases. She lives in St. Louis, Missouri.